LifeLight

"In Him was life, and the life was the light of men." John 1:4

Prayer

LEADERS GUIDE

CONCORDIA PUBLISHING HOUSE • SAINT LOUIS

3558 S. Jefferson Ave., St. Louis, MO 63118-3968
1-800-325-3040 • www.cph.org

Written by Mark Stirdivant

Edited by Brian Chisamore

Field testing coordinated by Lavern Schmidt

Cover illustration by Andrea Eberbach

This publication may be available in braille, in large print, or on cassette tape for the visually impaired. Please allow 8 to 12 weeks for delivery. Write to Lutheran Blind Mission, 7550 Watson Rd., St. Louis, MO 63119-4409; call toll-free 1-888-215-2455; or visit the Web site: www.blindmission.org.

Manufactured in the United States of America

1 2 3 4 5 6 7 8 9 10 20 19 18 17 16 15 14 13 12 11

Contents

Introduction

Welcome to LifeLight

A special pleasure is in store for you. You will be instrumental in leading your brothers and sisters in Christ closer to Him who is our life and light (John 1:4). You will have the pleasure of seeing fellow Christians discover new insights and rediscover old ones as they open the Scriptures and dig deep into them, perhaps deeper than they have ever dug before. More than that, you will have the pleasure of sharing in this wonderful study.

LifeLight—An In-depth Study

LifeLight is a series of in-depth Bible studies. The goal of LifeLight is that through a regular program of in-depth personal and group study of Scripture, more and more Christian adults may grow in their personal faith in Jesus Christ, enjoy fellowship with the members of His body, and reach out in love to others in witness and service.

In-depth means that this Bible study includes the following four components: individual daily home study; discussion in a small group; a lecture presentation on the Scripture portion under study; and an enhancement of the week's material (through reading the enrichment magazine).

LifeLight Participants

LifeLight participants are adults who desire a deeper study of the Scriptures than is available in the typical Sunday morning adult Bible class. (Mid-to-older teens might also be LifeLight participants.) While LifeLight does not assume an existing knowledge of the Bible or special experience or skills in Bible study, it does assume a level of commitment that will bring participants to each of the nine weekly assemblies having read the assigned readings and attempted to answer the study questions. Daily reading and study will require from 15 to 30 minutes for the five days preceding the LifeLight assembly. The day following the assembly will be spent reviewing the previous week's study by going over the completed study leaflet and the enrichment magazine.

LifeLight Leadership

While the in-depth process used by LifeLight begins with individual study and cannot achieve its aims without this individual effort, it cannot be completed by individual study alone. Therefore, trained leaders are necessary. You fill one or perhaps more of the important roles described below.

The Director

This person oversees the LifeLight program in a local center (which may be a congregation or a center operated by several neighboring congregations). The director

- serves as the parish LifeLight overall coordinator and leader;
- coordinates the scheduling of the LifeLight program;
- orders materials;
- convenes LifeLight leadership-team meetings;
- develops publicity materials;
- recruits participants;
- maintains records and budgeting;
- assigns, with the leadership-team, participants to small discussion groups;
- makes arrangements for facilities;
- communicates outreach opportunities to small-group leaders and to congregational boards;
- follows up on participants who leave the program.

The Assistant Director *(optional)*

This person may assist the director. Duties listed for the director may be assigned to the assistant director as mutually agreeable.

The Lecture Leader

This person prepares and delivers the lecture at the weekly assembly. **(Lesson material for the lecture leader begins on p. 8.)** The lecture leader

- prepares and presents the Bible study lecture to the large group;

• prepares worship activities (devotional thought, hymn, prayer), using resources in the study leaflet and leaders guide and possibly other, outside sources;

• helps the small-group discussion leaders to grow in understanding the content of the lessons;

• encourages prayer at weekly leadership-team and discussion leaders meetings.

The Small-Group Coordinator *(optional; the director may fill this role)*

This person supervises and coordinates the work of the small-group discussion leaders. The small-group coordinator

• recruits with the leadership-team the small-group discussion leaders;

• trains or arranges for training of the discussion leaders;

• assists the director and discussion leaders in follow-up and outreach;

• encourages the discussion leaders to contact absent group members;

• participates in the weekly leadership-team and discussion-leaders equipping meetings;

• provides ongoing training and support as needed.

The Small-Group Discussion Leaders

These people guide and facilitate discussion of LifeLight participants in the small groups. **(Lesson material for the small-group leaders begins on p. 51.)** There should be one discussion leader for every group of no more than twelve participants. The small-group discussion leaders are, perhaps, those individuals who are most important to the success of the program. They should, therefore, be chosen with special care and be equipped with skills needed to guide discussion and to foster a caring fellowship within the group. These discussion leaders

• prepare each week for the small-group discussion by using the study leaflet and small-group leaders guide section for that session **(see p. 51)**;

• read the enrichment magazine as a study supplement;

• guide and facilitate discussion in their small group;

• encourage and assist the discussion group in prayer;

• foster fellowship and mutual care within the discussion group;

• attend weekly discussion leaders training meetings.

Leadership Training

LifeLight leaders will meet weekly to review the previous week's work and plan the coming week. At this session, leaders can address concerns and prepare for the coming session. LifeLight is a 1½-hour program with no possibility for it to be taught in the one hour typically available on Sunday mornings. Some congregations, however, may want to use the Sunday morning Bible study hour for LifeLight preparation and leadership training. In such a meeting, the lecture leader and/or small-group coordinator may lead the discussion leaders through the coming week's lesson, reserving 5 or 10 minutes for problem solving or other group concerns.

While it requires intense effort, LifeLight has proven to bring great benefit to LifeLight participants. The effort put into this program, both by leaders and by participants, will be rewarding and profitable.

The LifeLight Weekly Schedule

Here is how LifeLight will work week by week:

1. Before session 1, each participant will receive the study leaflet for session 1 and the enrichment magazine for the course. The study leaflet contains worship resources (for use both in individual daily study and at the opening of the following week's assembly) and readings and study questions for five days. Challenge questions will lead those participants who have the time and desire a greater challenge into even deeper levels of study.

2. After the five days of individual study at home, participants will gather for a weekly assembly of all LifeLight participants. The assembly will begin with a brief period of worship (5 minutes). Participants will then join their assigned small discussion groups (of twelve or fewer, who will remain the same throughout the course), where they will go over the week's study questions together (55 minutes). Assembling together once again, participants will listen to a lecture presentation on the readings they have studied in the previous week and discussed in their small groups (20 minutes). After the lecture presentation, the director or another leader will distribute the study leaflet for the following week. Closing announcements and other necessary business

may take another five minutes before dismissal.

In some places some small groups will not join the weekly assembly because of scheduling or other reasons. Such groups may meet at another time and place (perhaps in the home of one of the small group's members). Those congregations may record the lecture given by the lecture leader at the weekly assembly and duplicate it for use by other groups meeting later in the week.

3. On the day following the assembly, participants will review the preceding week's work by rereading the study leaflet they completed (and that they perhaps supplemented or corrected during the discussion in their small group) and by reading appropriate articles in the enrichment magazine.

Then the LifeLight weekly study process will begin all over again!

Recommended Study and Worship Resources

The Lutheran Study Bible. St. Louis: Concordia Publishing House, 2009. This resource contains more than 26,000 study and application notes, a most thorough reference guide (pp. lxv–cx), and over 90,000 cross-references, as well as a 31,000-entry concordance, maps, charts, and timelines.

Concordia Self-Study Bible, New International Version. St. Louis: Concordia Publishing House, 1986. Interpretive notes on each page form a running commentary on the text. The book includes cross-references, a 35,000-word concordance, full-color maps, charts, and timelines.

Roehrs, Walter R., and Martin H. Franzmann. *Concordia Self-Study Commentary*. St. Louis: Concordia Publishing House, 1979. This one-volume commentary on the Bible contains 950 pages and is tailored for lay use.

The Concordia Organist. St. Louis: Concordia Publishing House (order no. 99-2264). A 31-CD collection of pipe organ accompaniments for all the hymns and liturgical music in *Lutheran Service Book*. Use these CDs for worship hymn accompaniment.

Every Voice a Song Pipe Organ Accompaniment for 180 Hymns and Liturgy. St. Louis: Concordia Publishing House (order no. 99-1565). Use this music CD for worship hymn accompaniment.

Prayer's True Foundation

Selected Passages

Preparing for the Session

Central Focus

Prayer is a common spiritual topic these days. Prayer is best seen primarily as a God-given gift bestowed upon the baptized Christian, and not a mere legalistic duty by which we can get what we want out of God. Jesus' own example provides us a valuable window into what He intends for our life of prayer.

Objectives

That participants, led by the Holy Spirit working through God's Word, will

1. learn the baptismal ground and wellspring of prayer;
2. recognize prayer as a gift and privilege rooted in God's command; and
3. find the scriptural basis for confidence when they pray to the heavenly Father.

Note for the small-group leaders: Lesson notes and other materials you will need begin on page 51.

For the Lecture Leader

Session Plan

Worship

Begin the session with the hymn printed in the study leaflet. Accompaniments are available in denominational hymnals, such as *Lutheran Service Book* or *Lutheran Worship* (refer to hymnal index). (Note: Concordia Publishing House has available *The Concordia Organist.* All the initial worship hymns in the LifeLight courses are included in this resource. It's especially helpful for mission congregations and small parishes. See the list of study resources on p. 7.) Follow with this prayer:

Prayer

Heavenly Father, we thank You for the privilege of prayer. We dare to approach Your holy throne only because of Your command, promise, and encouragement. You have washed us in Holy Baptism, making us Your true children, conformed to the image of Your own dear Son. Grant us confident faith so that we may pray in Christ's name and fulfill our holy calling. Amen.

Lecture Presentation

1 Baptismal Foundation (Galatians 3:23–29; Hebrews 10:19–22)

You have embarked on a study of prayer. The journey will cover a good amount of familiar ground, because prayer is not just for the advanced, well-studied Christian. Right from the very beginning, a believer is taught by God's Word to pray. On the box of a board game called *Othello* is its simple slogan: "A minute to learn . . . a lifetime to master." While it may seem true that prayer is also an easy-to-learn skill, we find out early on that it is always a gift of God, a high privilege that is noble in its simplicity and all-encompassing as it penetrates into our life. The more you study it from God's Word, the more you realize how much you have to learn about prayer and how to pray. It truly takes a lifetime to master!

Prayer touches on every other topic of theology, but most especially does it rely on, and flow from, the doctrine of justification, which is the center of the Christian faith. This doctrine can be simply stated as this: God gives grace, blessings, and forgiveness to us all because of Jesus Christ and nothing else. Baptism is not an addendum to our justification. Instead, one's Baptism is the divinely bestowed moment when grace, blessings, and forgiveness become the certain possession of the lost and condemned person. This blessed sacrament also grants to the new believer the privilege to call upon the Lord in prayer. The washing of water and the Holy Spirit bestows an inheritance going back to Abraham, no matter whether you are Jew or Greek, slave or free, male or female.

Here's how it does that: at Baptism, the triune name of God was placed upon you, along with all the mighty works and promises that He attaches to His name. You put on Christ as a garment, as Paul teaches (Galatians 3:27), and prayer is part of what you're getting all "dressed up" for. As you pray, the hand of the saving faith that has been created in your heart by the Holy Spirit takes hold of all the blessings and gifts that your Father gives to you through His Son. The regular practice of prayer puts all of the realities inherent in Baptism to work in your everyday life. Martin Luther was known to emphasize the present tense rather than the past when speaking of this sacrament: not "I *was* baptized," but instead, "I *am* baptized into Christ!"

So a Bible study on the topic of prayer will look in many respects like a study that covers sanctification, the Christian life, or the believer's journey this side of heaven—a journey guided by the instruction, forgiveness, and encouragement of the Lord. And since Baptism is where He not only got that all started for you, but also where He renews that love and forgiveness each day, it is fitting that Baptism would also be the beginning of prayer, as well as its constant fountain. Whether we've done it all our lives or are only recently getting back into the practice, through prayer we respond to the encouragement given us in Hebrews (10:22) that says, "Let us draw near with a true heart in full assurance of faith, with our hearts sprinkled clean . . . and our bodies washed with pure water."

2 Joining the Royal Priesthood (1 Peter 1:3–9; 2:9; Exodus 19:5–6)

As we look a little closer into the privilege of prayer that is granted to us in Baptism, we find that this privilege indicates a new identity that we have received. Once, we were far away, separated from Christ and strangers to His promises. Now we have been brought near by His blood. That blood accomplished more for us than wiping our slate of sins clean; it also conferred upon us, in a certain manner of speaking, an ordination.

This "ordination," however, is different from the particular ceremony that publicly affirms a divine call and places a qualified man into the Office of the Holy Ministry. This "ordination" is intended for all people whom the Lord will call to faith in Christ, male or female, declaring the baptized to be a member of a royal priesthood. This new identity of the Christian as a priest is a significant part of the inheritance of which Paul spoke in Galatians 3. The Baptism liturgy (see *LSB*, p. 268) includes a part just before the signing of the cross where the pastor asks for the name of the person about to be baptized. The pastor does not ask this because he has forgotten the name and needs a reminder; no, this ceremony is meant to explain what Baptism does for us. Our old identity, in which we were sold into slavery to sin, no longer defines us, for we have been transferred from the realm of darkness into the light of Christ.

You may be familiar with the biblical phrase "born again." Jesus used these words when He was explaining Baptism to Nicodemus in John 3, and it is the term that Peter writes in the opening words to his first epistle: (1:3) "He (the Father) has caused us to be born again to a living hope through the resurrection of Jesus." Our Savior told the incredulous Nicodemus that he must experience this new birth in order to be saved; Peter emphasizes that it is totally the merciful work of God, completed in full for all people because Christ died on the cross and rose from the dead, and this birth is accomplished in the Christian as a gift of the Holy Spirit in Baptism. The "again" in "born again" is the Greek word *anothen*, which can also be translated "from above." Thus, the new birth is a new identity that comes to us from above, that is, solely from God Himself, without a prior requirement placed on us.

Along with the new identity comes a new calling, a holy vocation that befits the Christian as a royal priest. What did priests do in the Old Testament? They offered the sacrifices that the Lord specified; they interceded with God for the sake of His people; they were the go-betweens, possessing direct access to the throne of grace, which is the specific, promised location of almighty God's merciful presence. Of course, only one, the high priest, could once a year, on the Day of Atonement, walk between the overlapped curtains and sprinkle the blood on the cover of the ark, or mercy seat. But as Hebrews teaches, Christ has now done that task in full reality, achieving full atonement for all people, with no further need for repetition, and has bestowed His priestly go-between role upon all baptized believers, who are His priests. The sacrifices we offer do not involve animals; instead, we offer our very lives in service to Christ in our neighbor, and that includes praying for their every need, commending them directly to our heavenly Father.

3 Example of John and Jesus (Luke 11:1; John 3:25–31)

John the Baptist had a supporting role leading up to the grand entrance of the main character, Jesus the promised Messiah, the long-awaited Savior. He takes center stage in the season of Advent, complete in his signature costume of camel's hair and also in his eccentric diet of locusts and wild honey. Before they even hear a word, John's audience is captivated! Then he begins to speak his message: "Repent, for the kingdom of heaven is at hand." Thus he fulfills Isaiah's prophecy that refers to him as "the voice of one crying in the wilderness: 'Prepare the way of the Lord.'"

There are several things John did in his ministry to prepare God's people for the Christ. First among them, of course, would be his baptizing. The hearers confessed their sins and received forgiveness in and with the water applied by John's hand. When he told the crowds (including those whom he called a "brood of vipers") to produce fruit in keeping with repentance, he also instructed them as to their various life vocations. Depending on their calling, their new life of faith would take shape in a way that was tailor-made to the specific people whom they would serve or over whom God gave them authority. Tax collectors received a different answer to the question "What shall we do?" than did soldiers. John would make it clear that mercy toward one's neighbor is the ethos of one who is baptized for repentance, waiting for the coming of Christ.

But there is one other notable thing that John the Baptist taught people, presumably also in preparation for Jesus' coming. It is revealed by one of Jesus' disciples, who up to this point must have observed Him keeping a regular prayer practice. He finally gathered enough courage to ask the Lord to teach them to pray, and he pointed out specifically that he would like to learn how to pray "as John taught his disciples" (Luke 11:1). The Bible is silent on the exact form and content of John's prayer instructions, but there may be a point to that. Perhaps that's in line with John's own statements: "(His) sandals I am not worthy to carry" (Matthew 3:11) and "He must increase, but I must decrease" (John 3:30).

John had taught his disciples to pray because prayer is built on God's gift of Baptism, and it grows from the life journey of repentance that Baptism initiates. Jesus taught His disciples to pray not simply because they watched and followed His example, and not because one of them pestered Him to do it. Rather, prayer to God the Father is a privilege unique to Jesus, and it was His good pleasure to share that privilege with us.

4 The Command to Pray (Psalm 50:14–15; Matthew 6:5–8; Luke 18:1–8)

"Is it a sin if we do not pray?" I was caught flat-footed one Sunday morning with that question, just as the Divine Service was about to begin. There was no time for me to get out a good answer right then and there. I did not know from what perspective this question was asked. To me, it plopped in my lap right out of the blue.

Perhaps the sticky word in that question is "sin." When you talk about sin, you talk about the Law. You talk about punishments for breaking God's commandments. You depict the Lord acting in His "alien work," with His gavel raised, ready to hand down a relentless punishment. In dealing with the Law, there is no room to consider a loving, heavenly Father. That's part of the reason why I choked on that question.

How can threats, punishments, and condemnations be attached to a gift as precious as prayer? Wouldn't it be better to encourage people to pray by emphasizing its blessings, rather than by cajoling them with a negative attitude, raising the specter of sin if Christians don't do their duty? When a Christian prays, he is certainly not performing a work that saves him or improves his standing before God. A quick glance at Reformation history should render that fact unmistakable. Given what we've studied so far about prayer, it would be far better to consider it in light of the Gospel. Yet we hear about God's command to pray. What do we make of that?

Consider how Scripture answers this fundamental question in connection with the divine institution of Baptism. Christ Himself gave the command, (Matthew 28:19) "Go . . . make disciples . . . [by] baptizing." He laid out the simple fact that "whoever believes and is baptized will be saved" (Mark 16:16). When Paul was converted, he recalled Ananias linking together the commands to be baptized and to pray: (Acts 22:16) "Rise and be baptized and wash away your sins, calling on His name." These words may sound like a demand is being placed on us, until you hear the benefits of Baptism: "born of water and the Spirit"; "washing of regeneration"; "He saved us"; "He chose us"; "you will receive the gift of the Holy Spirit"; "this is not your own doing; it is the gift of God"; "the promise is for you and for your children . . . everyone whom the Lord our God calls" (John 3:5; Titus 3:5; Ephesians 1:4; Acts 2:38; Ephesians 2:8; Acts 2:39). Baptism is all about receiving a gift *passively*, without any prior works or requirements. Prayer, likewise, can be approached in the same way.

The command to pray is not to place another impossible burden on the Christian's shoulders; it is rather the other way around: it's God at work, setting up His divinely ordained avenue to cast our burdens on Him. His command is in place to ensure that prayer as His gift to us will not ever be taken away. The hammer comes down not on us, but on the devil, the world, and our sinful flesh, the enemies who do not want us to pray and who do not want God's will to be done. "Call upon Me in the day of trouble"; "ask, and you will receive"; "intercessions . . . be made for all people"; "pray without ceasing"; "let your requests be made known to God"; "come to Me . . . and I will give you rest" (Psalm 50:15; John 16:24; 1 Timothy 2:1; 1 Thessalonians 5:17; Philippians 4:6; Matthew 11:28). These are all commands, but they are rich in the Gospel. Just as the command to baptize is a command to let the Good News of salvation be personally applied to people young or old, whether they look like you or not, so prayer is commanded to remove all doubt that your loving, heavenly Father would love for you to talk to Him at any time.

Is it a sin to spit in God's face and say that He can have His blessing because we want nothing of it? Absolutely—that's an expression of utter unbelief, just as it would be a sin to despise Baptism. Then in that case, the Law must condemn. But if you were given a million-dollar check, after you recover from fainting would you make a big deal about how you had to sign that check and how much of an effort it was to obey the bank's requirement and scribble your name on the back? Of course not! How much sillier it is to talk about the extent of our obedience when it comes to the infinitely valuable gift of prayer!

5 God's Promise to Hear (Luke 11:9–13; Psalm 91; Philippians 4:19)

It's pretty common knowledge all around Protestant Christianity that we don't pray to the saints. What some people are surprised to hear is that the reason that saints are not invoked has to do with more than just idolatry. It's pretty easy to draw the line from "You shall have no other gods" to rule out the act of prayer to anyone but the Holy Trinity. We should obey this commandment with all our heart so we do not bring the Lord's just judgment on our heads. But that's only the Law reason why we don't pray to the saints. In true Lutheran fashion, we must also see what the Gospel has to say about it.

The Augsburg Confession of 1530 says it very well: "Our churches teach that the history of saints may be set before us so that we may follow the example of their faith and good works, according to our calling. . . . But the Scriptures do not teach that we are to call on the saints or to ask the saints for help. Scripture sets before us the one Christ as the Mediator, Atoning Sacrifice, High Priest, and Intercessor [1 Timothy 2:5–6]. He is to be prayed to. He has promised that He will hear our prayer" (XXI 1–3 in *Concordia: The Lutheran Confessions*, second edition [St. Louis: Concordia Publishing House, 2006]).

The point here is this: God has provided a great and all-encompassing promise to hear and answer prayer. Prayer to Him is so all-sufficient that one does not need to look to saints or any other source for help and comfort. The Christian finds all he needs in Jesus Christ the Savior and in everything that He has done for us. Our heavenly Father is pleased to hear His children call upon Him, and He will deliver according to His rich promises.

Jesus argues from the lesser to the greater in Luke 11:11–13: "What father among you, if his son asks for a fish, will instead of a fish give him a serpent . . . ? If you then, who are evil, know how to give good gifts to your children, how much more will the heavenly Father give the Holy Spirit to those who ask Him!" We earthly parents couldn't presume to love our children to a greater extent than God the Father does; in comparison to His perfect holiness, we are nothing but evil. Yet we still obey our God-given instinct to give good things to our little ones, and that assures us that He will respond to our prayers with all the more love and compassion. We are confident He truly will supply our every need according to His riches in glory in Christ.

Conclusion

Prayer is based on Baptism. It is a gift bestowed along with all the other privileges that are granted to the Christian as a royal priest. The Lord's command to pray is best understood as an act of grace coupled with His promise to hear our prayer.

Concluding Activities

Conclude the session with an appropriate prayer and distribute the study leaflet for week 2.

Prayer's Liturgical Shape

Selected Passages

Preparing for the Session

Central Focus

This lesson will explore the rich treasure that a liturgical heritage brings to prayer. From psalms to catechism to the Sunday Divine Service and the seasons of the Church Year, we have a wealth of material from which we can construct our own daily prayer routine.

Objectives

That participants, led by the Holy Spirit working through God's Word, will

1. analyze and employ the historic liturgy's collect structure;

2. utilize the Psalter for prayer's structure and content; and

3. construct a daily prayer practice that stems from the Church's worship life together.

Note for the small-group leaders: Lesson notes and other materials you will need begin on page 55.

For the Lecture Leader

Session Plan

Worship

Begin the session with the hymn printed in the study leaflet. Accompaniments are available in denominational hymnals, such as *Lutheran Service Book* or *Lutheran Worship* (refer to hymnal index). (Note: Concordia Publishing House has available *The Concordia Organist.* All the initial worship hymns in the LifeLight courses are included in this resource. It's especially helpful for mission congregations and small parishes. See the list of study resources on p. 7.) Follow with this prayer:

Prayer

O Holy Spirit, You call, gather, enlighten, and sanctify the Church, keeping us united in the faith. Grant that the words You teach us in worship would guide our prayers wherever we may be, for we acknowledge by faith that these are the divine words of life. Amen.

Lecture Presentation

1 Prayers at Church: Collects (Psalm 122; Acts 2:42; Ephesians 5:19–20)

The faithful heart rejoices to set foot in the Lord's house of worship. Whether it is the Hebrew pilgrim of ancient days making the yearly ascent to the holy temple in Jerusalem or our congregation's newest member, each one declares his or her inmost song in the words of Psalm 122: "I was glad when they said to me, 'Let us go to the house of the Lord!'" And what is it that makes you glad? More than the friends, the coffee, the donuts, or even the great hymns, there is Almighty God, the One who gathers you together as His Church to receive blessings from His shining face.

After Peter gave his sermon at Pentecost in the second chapter of Acts, Luke describes a busy, active Church, with believers going about the activities commanded them by their Lord. "The prayers" in Acts 2:42 suggest certain learned prayers or petitions. The Psalms themselves had been used for centuries even prior to this point, and other liturgical recitations are evident among the earliest Christians. For instance, consider Philippians 2:6–11 or 1 Timothy 3:16 (some say these are creedal fragments; others believe they were early hymns or even possibly the "spiritual songs" mentioned in Ephesians 5:19). Then as now, prayers were not only private moments with God, using words that come spontaneously from the heart (you may have heard of the Latin term *ex corde*), but the prayers were also finely crafted liturgical gems offered by the congregation in public worship.

A specific form of structured prayer that is used in the Divine Service and at other times of public congregational gathering is called the collect (KAH–lekt). The Collect for the Day is the prayer that was designed to fit with the Propers, that is, the Scripture readings and other variable portions of the service that are assigned by the Church Year calendar or lectionary for each particular Sunday or festival day. True to its name, this liturgical prayer in a way "collects" together in one central idea all the themes, emphases, and divine gifts that the Scripture readings are proclaiming that day, and then makes a request of the Lord on the basis of that one main point. Take notice of the Collect for the Day, and you might receive significant assistance in retaining something truly meaningful that you can take home with you after church.

When you hear the pastor pray a collect on behalf of all (and when praying along with him, of course), listen for the five distinct elements found in collects: [*this may be written on a board, if available*]

1. **God's Name**—a scriptural name that God has ascribed to Himself and bids us to use when we call upon Him in prayer. Most collects are prayed to the Father. However, since in the Trinity no person is greater or less than another, addressing a prayer to the Son, the Holy Spirit, or God in His triune nature is also appropriate.

2. **Reason**—a scriptural promise or deed that the Lord has provided us as a rationale for us to approach Him in this particular prayer. This part of the collect format teaches us very clearly that we ask for what He has already provided or guaranteed, and it strengthens the Christian's confidence to stand before His throne.

3. **Petition**—the request that is clearly stated as the heart of the collect. Since the collect is drawn from Scripture, this request is in accord with God's will rather than our own.

4. **Result**—related to the last two elements, this is sometimes introduced with "so that . . ." It says what we can expect will happen when our heavenly Father performs that for which the petition asks. Sometimes the reason or result elements are left implied in the collect.

5. **Termination**—a conclusion to the prayer, often using the words "through Jesus Christ our Lord," which recalls the promise of Jesus in John 16:23. The "full termination" of a collect is an ascription of praise to Christ, who, following His resurrection, lives and reigns now and forever as one God together with the Father and the Holy Spirit.

2 The Church Year and Prayer (Psalm 77:10–15; Deuteronomy 5:15; Matthew 12:6–8)

The Church's yearly liturgical cycle has Sunday as its most basic building block. Called the "first day of the week" in the Easter Gospel narratives, Sunday serves as a continuing weekly proclamation of the resurrection of our Lord, no matter what time of the year it is. The Third Commandment may say "Remember the Sabbath day," but its meaning in the Catechism clarifies that no day of worship is absolutely required, but rather that we hold God's Word sacred and not despise the preaching of the Gospel. That being said, there are still very good reasons why Sunday should retain its traditional, honored place as the day of Christ's visit among us in Word and Sacrament.

As mentioned earlier, for each Sunday, the liturgical schedule of readings, or lectionary, gives specific readings from the Psalms, another Old Testament book, an Epistle, and one of the four Gospel books. The last selection is given a certain prominence in the Sunday Divine Service in that the Holy Gospel consists of words spoken from the mouth of Jesus Christ Himself, or a narrative describing one of the events in His incarnation, ministry, death, and resurrection that has been handed down to us by those whom the Holy Spirit inspired. The theme that is drawn from these Scripture readings sets the tone not only for the Sunday service but also for the devotional and prayer life of God's people as they go forth during the rest of the week to their homes and vocations.

The weekly rhythm of Sundays receives further shape and direction when combined with the various Church Year seasons. The central themes of Christ's person and work, namely His incarnation, death, and resurrection, are highlighted in the two highest festival seasons of the year, Christmas and Easter. I say they are festival *seasons* because it takes more than a single observance to get in all that the corresponding theme has to offer. Prayers of the faithful can include the specific emphases that are brought forward by the different seasons and their lectionary readings. Here is where the Collect for the Day that is particular to each Sunday and festival day in the Church Year can be quite practical: this portion of the Divine Service liturgy conveniently supplies that theme upon which other prayers may be built.

The Christmas and Epiphany seasons link the great miracle of the Word made flesh to His continuing life in and with the Church, all the while heralding the continual spread of the Gospel to all nations. In the Easter season, the focus is on the hidden glory of our Lord's crucifixion, His magnificent triumph over death, and the promise of our own resurrection of the flesh on the Last Day. Advent and Lent each serve in their own unique ways as penitential seasons in which we prepare for the joyous upcoming feast with a time of intense study of God's Word, confession of our sin, and prayer. The Pentecost season, or Time of the Church, is designed for the Christian to draw strength from both the person and work of Jesus for a life of faith and prayer. There are countless occasions and opportunities to pray, thanks to the variety of the whole counsel of God that is preached during the seasons of the Church Year.

3 Psalms—the Bible's Prayers (Psalm 98:1–3; Colossians 3:16)

The apostle Paul literally commands the indwelling of the Word of Christ among the Christians in Colossae. Together with the necessary teaching and admonishing in all wisdom, he is eager to include singing God's Word in three distinct forms as the desired outward signs of its taking up residence in the believers' hearts. And of those three forms of singing mentioned, the Psalms take first place. As the Bible's own collection of prayers, the Psalter (or Book of Psalms) should receive special consideration as we consider in depth the topic of prayer. Whether you sing or chant a psalm following an intricate tune, speak it back and forth to one another, or silently pray and meditate on just a few of its words, these inspired prayers will prove their value to you over and over, no matter what your age, mood, background, or experience in faith may be.

The Psalms are poetry, and the main feature that most of them possess is a kind of "rhyme." But rather than matching sounds like the poetry to which we are typically accustomed, these divinely inspired masterpieces employ a rhyming of ideas known as parallelism. One line expresses a thought, and the next line repeats that same thought in similar or inverted words. Or it might strengthen or extend the thought; or even state an opposite or inverse thought than that of the preceding line. Other psalms, most notably Psalm 136, have a constantly repeating response line that is sung in a back-and-forth (or antiphonal) fashion. Parallelism is the perfect format for scriptural poetry because, as author C. S. Lewis pointed out, this feature does not drop out once you translate the psalm into another language. They may have originated in Hebrew, but the Psalms keep their basic literary feature intact, no matter what language is used when they are prayed. Take a look at Psalm 98, for instance, and see how in verse 2 the second line repeats and expands upon the first.

When using psalms for meditation and prayer, in addition to noting the parallel thoughts, you could also look for various genres, or types, of psalms and how they were employed in the prayers and worship of ancient Israel. Psalms of praise, such as 148, are joyful songs to the Lord for certain works that He has done. There are also worship or liturgy psalms, such as 24, and the "Songs of Ascents" (120–134), which bring the faithful confession of God's people together over many centuries. The psalms of lament, such as 77, are valuable prayers that the Christian may pray when oppressed by trials and the cross. A little stronger still are a few psalms of imprecation, most notably 137, which may make us squirm a little when we hear them today, but are probably best explained in light of Romans 12:19: "Vengeance is Mine, I will repay, says the Lord." Psalms of comfort, such as the popular Twenty-third Psalm, encourage us to rest secure in the everlasting peace of Christ, our Savior. There are also psalms that are appropriate for morning (5), evening (141), and personal confession (51). You may find other suggestions in your devotional materials for psalms to sing and pray; or, just as well, you could work your way through all 150 of them!

For millennia, the Psalms have been the prayers of God's people in all situations, the pinnacle of sacred poetry, and the faithful companion for the distraught when all other words had seemed worthless. Your Lord has preserved for you an inestimable treasure, found right in the middle of your Bible!

4 Using the Bible and the Catechism for Prayer (2 Timothy 3:14–17; Psalm 119:164)

Prayer is talking to God. No doubt you've heard that. But it may surprise you that God's chosen means of talking to us can easily be neglected when it comes to prayer. We have already found that prayer has its foundation in the promises of God our heavenly Father, and that our motivation to pray is born from our status in His kingdom as baptized royal priests. There is nowhere else that we can find these promises tied to the mighty acts of God for us than in the Scriptures. The psalmist writes that he praises the Lord seven times a day (119:164), not because it is a drudgery, or on account of some requirement laid upon him, but because he has discovered within God's "righteous rules" the precious

Gospel that gives him life, salvation, and comfort.

So, since the Bible is sufficient and profitable so that we may be "competent, equipped for every good work" (2 Timothy 3:17), which would include prayer, what role would the Catechism play? The Catechism simply teaches Scripture according to Scripture. It repeats for us what the Bible itself considers to be its most significant and foundational teachings. The explanations of main parts such as the Ten Commandments and the Creed are just as useful to induce prayer as the meanings of the petitions of the Lord's Prayer. Luther himself admitted to praying the Catechism, studying it, and repeating it word for word just like a child, along with psalms and well-known verses that he could recite by heart. So that's why confirmation class had all that memorization—it is intended as a prayer resource!

Martin Luther was no disconnected, ivory-tower-style theologian. He genuinely loved the people who heard his teaching and instruction. In an excellent tract written by Luther as a response to a request by none other than his barber, "Master" Peter Beskendorf, the great reformer explained in detail how he disciplined himself to pray while studying Scripture. (This tract can be found in *Luther's Works*, the American Edition, vol. 43, pp. 193–211.) You can't help but smile when reading how Luther connects the concentration that is necessary for a barber to cut hair to the same close attention that is needed while praying.

In this letter to Master Peter, Luther begins with the Catechism, picking out one specific point that it teaches and then building a four-stranded prayer upon it. He first asks, What does this piece of scriptural truth teach me? Then he offers thanks to God for His gifts that are inherent in this truth. Following that, he says, the Christian ought to confess his sin of unbelief in thoughts, words, or deeds in relation to the topic at hand. Luther's fourth strand of prayer is to offer a request to the Lord based on that teaching.

Taking the example of the Fourth Commandment, we begin Luther's four strands by noting that we are taught in this part of the Catechism to honor our father and mother. Specifically, we could meditate on the word *honor* as an additional requirement to simple obedience. We then thank God for the gift of parents and authorities and the high honor we have to be graced with such a blessing from His hand. As a confession, we could pour out before the Lord that we have taken our parents for granted or despised them so that they were dishonored by what we did or neglected to do. Confident in our heavenly Father's forgiveness freely given in Christ, we would then, in the fourth strand, offer our request that God would help us keep this commandment in the various ways through which we can demonstrate honor to the authorities the Lord has placed over us. Since Luther's time, there has emerged a very close parallel prayer structure to this, using the widely-known acronym ACTS: Adoration, Confession, Thanksgiving, and Supplication. Whichever order you choose, with a little practice, you could begin with the Catechism and easily move to any article of doctrine that you find in the Bible.

5 Putting Together a Daily Prayer Discipline (2 Samuel 24:24–25; Daniel 6:10; Jude 20–21)

All right. You can talk until you're blue in the face about how important prayer is, and you can discuss several ideas and forms for prayer. But in the end, it gets down to this: how do I get started, and how do I keep going in the exercise of prayer in my life? Whatever devotional resource that you consult, the important thing to look for first is a lectionary that is easy to follow. The Scripture readings, whether they skip around or go straight through the books in order, should incorporate a balance of books from different parts of the Bible. Don't forget to include the Psalter, with all the various prayers and praises that you can find there.

Another important matter is choosing a time to pray. It may be first thing in the morning, or just before bed, but it needs to be made a part of your regular routine, unique to yourself. Distractions, even cultural "staples" like television and the Internet, must be minimized. Don't be afraid to build up slowly your time allotted, or to try various strategies and resources, as long as you are directed to the Shepherd's green pastures and cool-water springs of His Word. One time you could devote your time to a simple reading and prayer by yourself, as Jesus suggests in Matthew 6:6. Another time, you might find it more appropriate to sing a hymn with your family and review with them in prayer and mutual confession and consolation the activities of the day.

You could review other parts of the Sunday liturgy, such as the Collect for the Day or the special petitions of the Prayer of the Church; include in your own prayers the people whose needs are brought before the Lord at your congregation's altar. When another Sunday approaches, you could prepare by reading the Scripture lessons that will shape the theme of that Divine Service. Choose something to do and stick to it for a while, to see how it works. Should you keep a journal? Perhaps, and it's worth trying out for yourself, but if writing is not a particular gift of yours, the rigor may discourage rather than invigorate, which is its true intent. Just like putting together an exercise routine, a prayer discipline takes work, but it's worth it. Keep in mind Luther's advice that to prepare for an especially busy day, one must pray more rather than less, and realize that, since we often have the opposite inclination, we must have plenty more to learn about in the realm of prayer discipline.

Conclusion

The liturgical resources for prayer are endless and can seem a little daunting. The Psalms, Catechism, and Scripture readings from the Church Year lectionary serve as excellent starting points. Various suggested structures for prayer abound, but we looked in depth at two tried-and-true possibilities. [*Perhaps you could share with your group some ideas for prayer that you have found helpful.*]

Concluding Activities

Conclude the session with an appropriate prayer and distribute the study leaflet for week 3.

Prayer's True Power

Selected Passages

Preparing for the Session

Central Focus

We now begin to look more closely at the Lord's Prayer itself and apply each petition to all prayers that we may offer. We pray to hallow God's name because it was His name that was placed upon us Christians at our Baptism. His kingdom comes not because we ask for it or bring it about by our efforts, but because He has promised us His Holy Spirit, who enables us to believe, live, and pray.

Objectives

That participants, led by the Holy Spirit working through God's Word, will

1. connect God's triune name to the Father's commands and promises for prayer;
2. recall the Holy Spirit's work in creating and sustaining the faith in believers; and
3. distinguish between the theologies of glory and of the cross, the secular and sacred kingdoms.

Note for the small-group leaders: Lesson notes and other materials you will need begin on page 59.

For the Lecture Leader

Session Plan

Worship

Begin the session with the hymn printed in the study leaflet. Accompaniments are available in denominational hymnals, such as *Lutheran Service Book* or *Lutheran Worship* (refer to hymnal index). (Note: Concordia Publishing House has available *The Concordia Organist*. All the initial worship hymns in the LifeLight courses are included in this resource. It's especially helpful for mission congregations and small parishes. See the list of study resources on p. 7.) Follow with this prayer:

Prayer

O Almighty God, Father, Son, and Holy Spirit, we thank You for granting us in our Baptism the power of Your name. Increase Your kingdom among us so that we believe Your Holy Word and lead a godly life, now and forever, through Christ Jesus our Lord. Amen.

Lecture Presentation

1 Our Father: Praying with Christ and Church (John 14:6–7; Isaiah 63:7, 16)

God is our true Father because He created us. He is the source of all our life and "in Him we live and move and have our being" (Acts 17:28). This is something we share with all people, regardless of faith, and it motivates in part the Church's mission to preach the Gospel to all of creation (Mark 16:15). But creation isn't the whole story. The right to call God our Father was forfeited when Adam and Eve rebelled against the Lord in the Garden of Eden. Sin planted an impassable gulf between heaven and earth and set us at odds with our Creator and with one another. The promise of Christ our Savior, which was announced immediately to our first parents (Genesis 3:15), brings with it the restoration of the right and invitation to pray. Notice that it is after that first Gospel promise that Moses informs us, "At that time people began to call upon the name of the Lord" (Genesis 4:26). Faith is given first, and then with that faith comes the privilege of prayer. Without faith in the Lord's salvation, paid for by the blood of Jesus, prayer is as impossible as pole-vaulting across the Grand Canyon.

As we found out earlier in this study, our Baptism places faith in our heart, which can then call upon God our heavenly Father. By His grace, extended to us in Christ Jesus, the Creator restored the relationship that was broken by us creatures. We did not seek out the Lord, but He sought us. Before faith came to us through Baptism, we could not have even summoned God to come into our heart. We can say "our Father" in our prayer because Christ earned for us all His rights that belong to Him as Son. Thanks to the Spirit of the Son in our hearts, we pray together with Him so that our prayer is His, and His is ours. Through our baptismal unity with Jesus Christ, we participate in the closest relationship described in the Bible, the mysterious relationship of the Holy Trinity. Our Savior said it Himself: (John 14:9) "Whoever has seen Me has seen the Father."

Christ also told us that He didn't come just to give us instructions on how we can access our heavenly Father in prayer in the same way that He did. His example in prayer was much more than modeling behavior that He wanted to see in us. He came not to show the way for us, as the disciple Thomas thought, but actually to *be* for us "the way, and the truth, and the life. No one comes to the Father except through Me" (John 14:6). By His perfectly united divine and human natures, Jesus, our risen Lord, is with us, and He is with the Father, so therefore, we, too, are with the Father through faith in Christ. The Church, called to faith by the Holy Spirit, is united with one another and with the Lord.

That's the other side of the "Our" in "Our Father." Whether we pray the Lord's Prayer alone or in unison with the largest crowd imaginable, the proper invocation remains "Our Father." Can private, personal prayer ever be appropriate? Sure it can. Peter's quick petition on the storm-tossed sea was "Lord, save me" (Matthew 14:30). But before you know it, your longing prayer as an isolated individual, buffeted by waves of trials, is answered by the Lord of the Church as He places you back in the boat with fellow forgiven sinners. You are not alone. You have your heavenly Father; you have Christ your Savior; you have the Holy Spirit, the Comforter; you have the family that God has provided for you; and you have the Holy Christian Church, the communion of saints. With that company of witnesses constantly surrounding you, you have renewed confidence to press forward with bold faith and speak to God as He truly is for you, calling Him, "Our Father."

2 The Power of God's Name (Exodus 3:13–15; Psalm 54; John 20:30–31)

Whether it's rendered as "Thou shalt not take the name of the LORD thy God in vain" or "You shall not misuse the name of the Lord your God," the Second Commandment automatically implies that there is a proper use of God's name. Along with that proper use comes the promise of great power to do the mighty works of the Lord. Breaking the Second Commandment—in any of the ways listed in the Catechism—means you are saying that you don't believe that God's name will work, that He won't come through for you as He promised.

Moses was unsure about God's power, and he had never heard God's name. So at the tender age of eighty, the prophet was treated to a pyrotechnic display without equal in the wilderness. Out of the burning bush, the Almighty God revealed His name for Moses: "I AM WHO I AM" (Exodus 3:14). His holy name is derived from this self-description, and in Hebrew it seems to be pronounced "Yahweh," although respect for God's powerful name produced a regular practice of saying "the LORD" whenever that name appeared in the reading of Scripture. This convention has carried over into most English translations, and in the Old Testament, when the word *LORD* appears in all capital letters, it indicates that the divine name is being used in the original language.

When Moses received the name of the Lord on Mount Sinai, he also received the power of God's name. Above his objections and pleas to "send someone else," God sent Moses to do what the Lord's name always does: save God's people. The Passover and Exodus would be the pivotal event of the entire Old Testament, having clear ties to the ultimate act of salvation, namely the death and resurrection of Jesus Christ. The nation of Israel for many generations would call on the name of the Lord with faithful remembrance of God's display of power against Pharaoh and how their ancestors were led out of Egypt. For example, Psalm 54:1 proclaims, "O God, save me by Your name, and vindicate me by Your might." The parallel structure of this verse informs us that the Lord's salvation is synonymous with vindication, and His name lines up with His might. The psalmist David is confident that when he calls on the Lord's name, he will be delivered, just as God has done in the past for His people.

This is the holy, divine name that Jesus claimed for Himself when He said, "Before Abraham was, I am" (John 8:58). The Jews who heard Him say this in the temple understood this claim of His so clearly that they picked up stones to punish what they thought was blasphemy. His miracles and teaching would give some demonstration that He possessed genuine power to save, but the full strength of vindication and forgiveness for people of all nations would not be revealed in unbridled glory; rather, it was hidden in the shame and horror of the cross. On Good Friday, the name of the Lord was pronounced in all its power in fulfillment of God's greatest promise to all of creation. On Easter, the resurrection of Jesus would proclaim life everlasting in His name. St. Paul assures us that when Jesus, who is the Lord, comes again, every knee shall bow at His name. And to think, you have for your own proper use that mighty name to call upon in prayer! You see, the true power of prayer is not found in your own fervent feeling or even in the strength of your faith. No, the power of prayer is in the name that is above every name, and it's backed by the Lord's own command and promise of salvation.

3 The Gift of the Holy Spirit (John 14:25–27; Joel 2:27–32; Luke 12:11–12)

Martin Luther had the insight to equate the coming of God's kingdom with the presence of the Holy Spirit. And, according to the Small Catechism, the two prongs of the Spirit's work among us involve our believing His Holy Word and living a godly life. Prayer fits in with both of these, and actually connects the two by the power and grace of the Holy Spirit. Faith inspired by the Spirit in the Christian's heart produces the fruit of good works, and all along the way, the believer draws the Spirit's strength through the Word that he has been called to believe. The Holy Spirit then moves the Christian to pray, building on that Word. Jesus calls the Spirit the Helper, or Comforter, and for what other purpose would He bring to our remembrance all that Jesus has said than for us to use His Words to pray to our Father? Since the chief work of the Holy Spirit is to point us to Christ, His help in our prayer recalls for us all the promises of God that are fulfilled in the words and works of our Lord Jesus.

When the Day of Pentecost arrived, and Peter preached his sermon to the assembled crowd (Acts 2), he cited the prophet Joel, who by inspiration had predicted the outpouring of the Holy Spirit. First, Jesus Himself would come, as Joel records God's words: (2:27) "You shall know that I am in the midst of Israel." Indeed, God walked in the flesh in the midst of His people, performing the great acts of salvation that from the very beginning He had promised to do. Just before His ultimate sacrifice on the cross and triumphant resurrection, and again before He ascended into heaven, Jesus made sure that His Church would be expecting the arrival of the Holy Spirit, who proceeds both from the Father and the Son. And the signs of that work of the Spirit among His gathered saints were not only going to be the spectacular miracles of tongues of fire and tongues of language. The prophecies, dreams, and visions that will be revealed to all flesh, male and female alike, along with all the fearful signs in heavens and earth, will serve one chief purpose: (v. 32) "And it shall come to pass that everyone who calls on the name of the Lord shall be saved." The Spirit helps God's people pray for their salvation. It's not that the prayer "earns" or "merits" the grace of the Lord; rather, it is the desired outcome of all divine work in the believer's heart to bring it to a full knowledge of all He has done. Since all of God's power is revealed in His name, as we have already seen, then the Holy Spirit directs us, once He has gathered us together with all believers in one Holy Christian Church, to call upon that name for all the blessings that the Father has promised.

Look for the Spirit's work to unfold in greater depth as we continue this study on prayer. He will constantly be pointing us to Christ, first to renew and strengthen our faith in His Holy Word, and then to encourage in us the proper fruit of faith, the godly life of good works "God prepared beforehand, that we should walk in them" (Ephesians 2:10). While we do well to maintain the biblical distinction between faith and works, the proper way to link them together is through prayer: we pray to increase and strengthen our faith, and we offer our priestly intercessions for everything and everyone pertaining to our God given vocations. It sounds like a daunting task, but remember St. Paul's comfort: (Romans 8:26) "We do not know what to pray for as we ought," but, "the Spirit helps us in our weakness."

4 The Theology of the Cross and the Theology of Glory (James 1:2–6; 1 Corinthians 15:19–24)

"Truly, You are a God who hides himself, O God of Israel, the Savior," sings the prophet Isaiah (45:15). God hides His earth-shattering glory from us, as He did for Moses in the cleft of the "Rock of Ages," (Exodus 33:21–23) so that we would not be destroyed by His utter holiness but, rather, saved through His boundless mercy. To reveal His true, loving nature toward sinners, God must be hidden in suffering and the cross. The theology of glory is the opinion of sinful man that not only must God make everything better for us just because we believe in Him, but that we should also conclude that we are doing something wrong if something bad is happening to us.

The theology of the cross is not easy to stomach. The tendency for us, no matter how mature our faith may be, is to think the opposite way. But this is not our unique problem. The apostle James was inspired to write comforting words to struggling Christians spread in many directions due to persecution. (1:2–3) "Count it all joy, my brothers," he says, "when you meet trials of various kinds, for you know that the testing of your faith produces steadfastness." Easy for him to say? It would be safe to say that in his leadership role in the Church in Jerusalem, James had plenty of trials that came his way. But rather than fret about a temporary lack or a compounding of sorrows, he counsels his fellow believers to "let steadfastness have its full effect"; that is, we should patiently rely on God's power, which is made perfect in weakness (2 Corinthians 12:9), in suffering, and in other things that are despised of the world. Understanding the hidden blessings in these adverse things requires divine wisdom that can only be requested through prayer.

The theology of glory may "feel" good and right to us, but in reality it is a mere house of cards. In 1 Corinthians 13:1, the apostle Paul tells us that the guarantee of temporal blessings alongside the preaching of the Gospel is just as much a "noisy gong or a clanging cymbal" as it is to speak truth without genuine love. It's not that we shouldn't be thankful for earthly things or be concerned about our brother's physical needs; James clearly teaches that in chapter 2, even though he condemns a worldly attitude in chapter 4. We bear one another's burdens, and we comfort our fellow believers especially when they begin to entertain the thought that God is punishing them. The key to rooting out a false theology of glory is to focus with joyful hearts on the resurrection of Christ. St. Paul warns, (1 Corinthians 15:19) "If in Christ we have hope in this life only, we are of all people most to be pitied." So we keep in mind what is emphasized very well in the Sundays toward the end of the Church Year: our time under suffering and the cross is temporary, and the true glory of Christ will be revealed to us not in our so-called "kingdom-building" efforts but rather at the end of the world, when the Lord will return again and every knee in heaven and on earth and under the earth shall bow before Him.

5 Prayer in Christ's Twofold Kingdom (Psalm 82; Zechariah 9:9; 1 Peter 2:13–25)

Pontius Pilate needed a simple, straightforward answer: "Are you the King of the Jews?" As Matthew, Mark, and Luke report, the only answer he receives (according to the Greek) is "You say." Not much of an answer, is it? Some translators, like those who produced the NKJV, try to make those two words into a complete sentence: "*It is as* you say," putting the words they added in italics. Others, as in the ESV, rephrase them as "You have said so." In John's Passion account, Jesus adds in response, (18:34) "Do you say this of your own accord, or did others say it to you about me?" So far, given these two mysterious responses, Pilate doesn't seem to be getting the answer he needed. He may have asked himself, Why is this man avoiding my question? The reason is revealed by Jesus Himself in verse 36: "My kingdom is not of this world."

But now, with this answer, *we* become the ones who are confused! Isn't it true that all authority and power in heaven and on earth belong to Christ? Aren't all the earthly kingdoms and "powers that exist" instituted by Him?

Jesus makes a distinction between the right-hand spiritual kingdom—that for which we pray in the Lord's Prayer—"Thy kingdom come"—and the left-hand secular kingdom. The first is one of faith and salvation, established by Christ's sacrifice and operating with forgiveness that's freely given. This is the kingdom that He said was not of this world. The second kingdom is one of order and law, established by God's gift of reason to man, operating through temporal punishments and rewards that are earned. It has nothing to do with forgiveness and eternal life. The heavenly Father grants blessings also in the worldly sphere, but they are secondary to those of the spiritual.

We cannot avoid either kingdom when it comes to the Christian life and prayer. We ask the Holy Spirit for His power to believe God's Word and live a godly life, and our Father gives us the world around us, including our particular vocations in it, to act in love toward our neighbor. The two kingdoms are kept distinct so that we don't stray into the theology of glory, but they work in harmony, as 1 Peter 2 describes. We serve our masters and leaders, and we pray for them, while at the same time, we proclaim the praises of Christ, who made us members of His holy kingdom.

Conclusion

The true power of prayer can be found in God's name and kingdom, as the Lord's Prayer teaches us in its introduction and first two petitions. We pray to our Father, along with Christ and our fellow Christians, calling on His name. He responds by sending us the Holy Spirit, establishing His spiritual kingdom of the Church among us, and sending us into the secular kingdom to serve our neighbor and pray for him in the name of Jesus.

Concluding Activities

Conclude the session with an appropriate prayer and distribute the study leaflet for week 4.

Prayer's Outcome: Thy Will Be Done

Selected Passages

Preparing for the Session

Central Focus

Our limited, human, and sin-plagued perspective can make it difficult to assess, and even accept, God's will. This lesson will not only shed light on what exactly it means to seek our Father's will, but it will also lead students to discover in Scripture how the Holy Spirit conforms our will to His.

Objectives

That participants, led by the Holy Spirit working through God's Word, will

1. discern properly what God's will is over against the will of the three spiritual enemies;
2. revisit the example of Jesus, specifically in His praying, "Thy will be done"; and
3. rejoice in the Spirit's work of keeping them steadfast in Word and faith.

Note for the small-group leaders: Lesson notes and other materials you will need begin on page 63.

For the Lecture Leader

Session Plan

Worship

Begin the session with the hymn printed in the study leaflet. Accompaniments are available in denominational hymnals, such as *Lutheran Service Book* or *Lutheran Worship* (refer to hymnal index). (Note: Concordia Publishing House has available *The Concordia Organist*. All the initial worship hymns in the LifeLight courses are included in this resource. It's especially helpful for mission congregations and small parishes. See the list of study resources on p. 7.) Follow with this prayer:

Prayer

Lord Jesus Christ, You once prayed in the Garden for our deliverance from sin, death, and Satan, using the petition "Thy will be done." Strengthen us as we follow You in our times of trial, that finally we may rejoice in full glory at the accomplishment of Your will for us by means of the cross. Amen.

Lecture Presentation

1 How Do You Find Out God's Will? (Hebrews 10:5–10; Romans 12:1–2)

Long ago, God made known His will at particular times using certain, tangible means. Gideon put his fleece on the ground, Moses had the burning bush, and the high priest could use the lots known as Urim and Thummim. Today we may envy these clear-cut, yes-or-no decision makers whereby God unmistakably made His will known to His people. We are told to pray for God's will, and we ask Him in the best way we can, but when do we become aware that He has given us His answer? Are we supposed to look for signs as they did in the Bible? Will the Lord speak to our hearts if we try hard to listen to His voice?

These questions are common today in much of the popular world of Christianity, but they make us Lutherans uncomfortable because they tend to steer our attention away from God's Word and Jesus Christ and have us focus instead on ourselves and our feelings. Even when we look in the Bible for direction, we can still be misled by our own conceptions of what God is saying in the words we read. When we fallen sinners start searching Scripture for direction in life, we gravitate to the Law, because that's the Word of God that addresses our actions. Then, the Law's condemnations crash down on our heads, and we end up either deceiving ourselves into saying we have no sin, or we become steeped in despair because we cannot escape the utter holiness of the almighty God.

That is why we need the Gospel as we look for our heavenly Father's will. The Good News of Jesus, our Savior, will not tell us what to do, but rather tells what our Lord has done for us. The only perfect fulfillment of God's holy will was accomplished for our sake in Christ's life, death, and resurrection. Everything He did and said was an act of salvation meant for forgiveness, help, and strength. When you meditate on any section of Scripture, that is, when you read it several times and say it repeatedly to yourself, remember first to thank God for the good He has given you through that passage or verse. That keeps the emphasis on the Gospel above everything else.

Once our souls are forgiven and restored with a heart that is now eager and willing to express love toward God and neighbor, we are enabled to see His Law in a new way. It may be called the "third use" of the Law (see Article VI of the Formula of Concord), but it isn't the Law that has changed into some different form. Rather, it is our perspective toward it that has changed. Now that the condemnation of the Law is removed from us through the sacrifice of Jesus, we can see our loving, heavenly Father's perfect will in the Ten Commandments. Where before there were only demands and punishments, now we will see ways in which we can serve Christ by serving our neighbor.

Our sinful nature inside of us has nothing to do with these invitations to love and faith—the flesh still needs compulsion and threats of punishments. But the new man, or renewed nature that we now possess—a right spirit that has been raised to life in us with Christ—rejoices at the teaching of God's Word and exalts His will. We got to this point not by agreeing to the Law or making a stronger commitment on our part to our Lord, but rather by trusting in His good gifts to us in Christ. He is the perfect fulfillment of God the Father's will. And as Hebrews declares: (10:10) "By that will we have been sanctified through the offering of the body of Jesus Christ once for all."

2 What If It's Not My Will? (Romans 7; Matthew 6:8; 2 Thessalonians 2:16–17)

"Wretched man that I am!" Paul cries out, echoing the same frustrations we have today. In writing Romans 7, he is not reminiscing over his life prior to his Christian conversion. Even after his total rebirth and renewal in the Holy Spirit through Baptism, the apostle admits that he constantly struggles with and yearns for rescue from "this body of death" (v. 24). And the same is true for us.

The sad truth for man on this earth is that, since the days of Genesis, "every intention of the thoughts of his heart was only evil continually" (6:5). The sin that Adam and Eve committed soon after the world's origin has produced in our own hearts an original sin that has corrupted our very will. Whenever our renewed spirit within us (the spirit that has been restored according to the image of God in Christ) calls obediently on the Lord in prayer, the sinful will never fails to stick its neck out and attempt to yank the believer back into self-serving idolatry. Many times, it succeeds.

The Christian who is well aware of this sinful inclination of the heart can feel a little uneasy when reading of God's acts of judgment on sinners and unbelievers. If you have ever been unsettled when hearing that in spite of all those plagues, the Lord hardened Pharaoh's heart, you are not alone. For one thing, God's hardening came as a result and confirmation of Pharaoh's consistent, stubborn hardening of his own heart. That is to say, at every opportunity, following each plague, the ruler of Egypt could have relented and allowed Moses to lead the people into freedom, but Pharaoh refused each time. In his case, the only divine judgment that fit was for the Lord to say, in effect: "Fine, have it your way."

But lest we despair and think along the lines of the theology of glory, we should beware of the tendency to believe that when we don't get what we pray for, it's because we have not been good enough or our faith or commitment to God is not strong enough. Even when you are not receiving the answer you want, your merciful Father still hears your prayer. You do not need to bargain your way out of a difficult situation, as if to say to Him, "I'll do *x* for You if You'll do *y* for me." Abraham may have boldly pleaded with the Lord for the deliverance of Lot, but he prayed with a humble heart, well aware of his beggar status. He did not approach God as an equal. Because the rescue of a faithful believer was in accord with the Father's will, Lot was spared, even though his home was destroyed and he had to flee. Then he mourned the loss of his wife, who had looked back in disobedience and turned into a pillar of salt. He had plenty to complain about! What assurance to know that our Lord's ways are higher than our ways! (Isaiah 55:9).

3 Praying in Gethsemane (Luke 22:39–46; Matthew 26:36–46; John 17)

The ultimate prayer of "Thy will be done" came from the lips of Jesus as He knelt with His face to the ground and prayed on the night He was arrested. You could almost depict this dramatic moment as the funnel through which is poured our every prayer that asks for God's will. Two scenes have Gethsemane as their backdrop: the Savior's times of prayer and His words to His sleeping disciples.

If you piece together the four Gospel accounts of this Holy Thursday evening, you notice that Jesus prays the High Priestly Prayer of John 17 immediately before He and the disciples cross over into the garden. In this rare window into the intimate communion between persons of the Holy Trinity, God the Son prays for the glorification of God the Father's name; for increasing faith, unity, and holiness of His disciples; and for those chosen out of the sinful world to believe through the apostolic message. He utters this prayer in the hearing of His disciples, so they would pray along with Him, that in their upcoming holy vocation as servants of the Word, many would believe and be united in Jesus.

After Jesus arrives in Gethsemane, he kneels down under the full weight of the burden that accompanies the prayer "Thy will be done." His drops of bloody sweat and His utter anguish prove that this petition does not consist of mere throwaway words. When Jesus says, "Not My will, but Yours, be done," He is not admitting guilt or weakness on His part. Instead, our Lord in His humiliated state is fully submitting Himself as a servant for our sakes to the eternal will of His Father. He completely fills up our righteousness and drowns our self-serving sinful will as easily as a candle is extinguished by the ocean.

Interspersed with our Lord's intense prayer sessions was His work to overcome for His disciples their temptation to give in to their own sorrow and exhaustion. His request had been for them to watch and pray along with Him; instead, they gave in to the weakness of the flesh. Christ's words to Peter, James, and John, with the rest of the disciples close by, are also a blessing to us as we pray for our heavenly Father's will to be done.

The prayer "Thy will be done" on the Mount of Olives involved a cup that the Father could not let pass from the lips of Jesus, our Savior. Drinking the cup meant going through the entire Passion experience for the salvation of the whole world. It was a bitter cup for Him to drink, because it was filled with the dregs of our disobedience. But once He drained it dry on nearby Calvary's hill, the cup of our Lord was now passed on to us, not as a cup of punishment or suffering, but as a cup of blessing, filled with forgiveness, grace, and life everlasting.

4 Three Enemies: What Their Will Is (1 Peter 5:8–9; Romans 7:14–25)

It has been called an "unholy trinity," not only because the devil, the world, and our sinful nature or flesh are completely opposed to God the Holy Trinity, but also because, just as the Godhead is fully united in one and the same essence and will, so also these three enemies are fully allied in an evil unity that is sworn to hinder, if possible, God's will among us. This joint attack does not feel pleasant, and according to the catechism, our heavenly Father graciously breaks and hinders it. Yet, ironically, it is also true that these three enemies are locked into doing nothing other than achieving God's will for His people.

Satan is at the center of this hideous alliance. His name means "accuser" or "prosecuting attorney," but not because he is interested in achieving justice. Instead, the ancient foe would rather twist God's Holy Word (especially the Law) into something that would destroy us. Peter warns us to look out for the devil as he prowls around like a roaring lion. The devil seeks someone to devour, not that he can take anything on his own, but he still does great damage by trying to convince the people of God that there is no hope, so that they are swallowed up by despair.

That's where the other two enemies come in. The sinful human nature is so much a corruption of the image of God. So instead of devoting oneself wholly out of love for others, the flesh is totally engulfed in gratifying oneself. Satan must have much easier work to do, thanks to the help of this ally. As John writes in his First Epistle, one of the key ways we can deceive ourselves is to say we have no sin. We engage in this deception either by arbitrarily softening God's Law or by comparing ourselves to others.

The sinful world is full of temptations and attacks. On one hand, our sinful nature gets tantalized by all the pleasures and vain things the world offers. Such vain things that sway men's hearts are revealed and denounced by the Book of Ecclesiastes. On the other hand, the world has always persecuted Christ, as well as His faithful people of all ages. But as Paul shows as he compares Ishmael and Isaac in Galatians 4, such persecution at the hands of the world is a small price compared to the greatness of God's promises that are always "yes" in Christ (2 Corinthians 1:20).

These enemies may be strong and formidable, but they are, in a favorite expression of Martin Luther, merely barking dogs on a chain, permitted to go no farther than our heavenly Father allows. As they attack, we can be confident they will also be yanked back by the collar at the time when it pleases God. When our sufferings at the hands of the devil, the world, and our flesh drive us to repentance and prayer, then these bitter enemies of the almighty God actually end up accomplishing His will!

5 Steadfast in His Word and Faith (1 Thessalonians 5:23–25; 1 Kings 19:13–18)

There are few things that the Christian can experience in life that are worse than when feeling as though God is not there. Suddenly, a heavy weight starts sinking down inside and there is a profound loneliness, even when family and friends are constantly near. If you've ever gone through this, you probably felt that the only reliable companions you had at that time were those three enemies—the devil, the world, and the flesh, with all their tricks and attacks robbing you of a moment's peace. But going to church and studying the Bible, which you knew in your head to be the very things you needed at that moment, were the two things your heart did not want to do.

These times can be scary for the Christian. Am I losing my faith? Did I ever truly believe in the first place? Has the Lord given up on me? If this is His will, then it doesn't seem all that advantageous to pray for His will to be done. Even close friends and family find it difficult to console someone who is in such a state. They may find it difficult to discern whether or not physiological concerns such as depression are also contributing factors. But they fear that to suggest professional help could make the problem worse.

While the work of counselors, psychiatrists, and other mental health professionals has a valuable place in the proper care of an individual, something more is needed to address deeper spiritual needs. The proper use of medications may be a godsend in making the necessary adjustments to one's emotions and harmful behaviors, but God's own spiritual medicine should not be overlooked. The apostle Paul gave a closing blessing to the Thessalonians that bestowed on these Christians, some of them weak and fainthearted, the presence of God Himself to make them sanctified. His peace grants wholeness to spirit, soul, and body, using these three terms to emphasize that the merciful Father extends His faithful care to every single part of His precious child. Paul also requests that they pray for him and for those with him. Not only is he urging them to perform their priestly duty of prayer, but he is also reminding all Christians that when they approach the Lord in prayer for others, an avenue is opened for Him to give also to them His strengthening Word and the Holy Spirit.

As we studied last week, the theology of the cross informs us that God works His true power in weakness and suffering. When the believer struggles with God's will as it is playing out in his life, the Father gives assurance and even more of His strength found in His Word. In fact, as the well-known "Footprints" story depicts, when we, His precious children, are in utter despair, then our Lord is nearer than ever, carrying us through difficulties and carrying out His good and gracious will.

Conclusion

God's will is not merely how He determines what happens to us, nor is it a question of whether we will fare well or poorly, depending on His whim. His will is for our salvation, and Jesus prayed for our sake in the Garden of Gethsemane. He actually used the very same words "Thy will be done" before drinking His assigned cup in full on Good Friday. When we are made aware of how our own will is contrary to His, then we can look to our Savior for a clean heart. With it, the Holy Spirit creates in us a will that is in conformity with that of our heavenly Father.

Concluding Activities

Conclude the session with an appropriate prayer and distribute the study leaflet for week 5.

Prayer's Nourishment for the Traveler

Selected Passages

Preparing for the Session

Central Focus

Daily bread is everywhere! As Luther pointed out, praying for it doesn't actually make it come to us, but rather our prayer leads us to realize that God provides us everything we need for this body and life. When we pay attention to the unique part that we play in the several roles of our Christian vocation, our hearts may be filled with genuine thanksgiving to our ever-provident God.

Objectives

That participants, led by the Holy Spirit working through God's Word, will

1. review all to which the phrase "daily bread" refers in their lives and how God provides it;

2. address any concerns about "selfishly" asking the Lord for daily bread; and

3. receive personal encouragement from what Scripture describes as Christian vocation.

Note for the small-group leaders: Lesson notes and other materials you will need begin on page 67.

For the Lecture Leader

Session Plan

Worship

Begin the session with the hymn printed in the study leaflet. Accompaniments are available in denominational hymnals, such as *Lutheran Service Book* or *Lutheran Worship* (refer to hymnal index). (Note: Concordia Publishing House has available *The Concordia Organist.* All the initial worship hymns in the LifeLight courses are included in this resource. It's especially helpful for mission congregations and small parishes. See the list of study resources on p. 7.) Follow with this prayer:

Prayer

Our Father in heaven, Your mercies are new every morning. You have provided everything, and for this we are grateful. Besides the richness of Your salvation, You have granted us every blessing in our daily life. Help us to realize this daily bread, receive it with thanksgiving, and share Your abundance with others who are in need of the mercy of Christ working through us, in whose name we pray. Amen.

Lecture Presentation

1 God Gives without Our Prayer (James 1:16–18; Romans 8:26–28)

So far, we have noticed that in the Lord's Prayer there has been attached to every one of the petitions a promise that has already been done: the Lord's name is hallowed, His kingdom comes, and His will is done on earth as it is in heaven—all before we utter a syllable to ask for it. This concept is fairly simple to grasp, once you consider that all of these petitions have been fulfilled in Christ. He has, by His work of salvation, inherited the name that is above every name. When He breathed out the Holy Spirit, Christ caused His spiritual kingdom to come as it does to this very day in the preaching of His Word and the administration of His Sacraments. In the garden, our Savior prayed, "Thy will be done," and so fulfilled that petition once and for all in our place. As Jesus Himself told His disciples, (Mark 11:24) "Whatever you ask in prayer, believe that you have received it, and it will be yours." He wasn't just offering a helpful tip on prayer that nobody before Him had ever considered. He was, in fact, the only one who could carry out that promise personally for every petition of the Lord's Prayer, as well as for all other prayers.

Now we come to daily bread. As the catechism teaches, that's all of our earthly stuff. Specifically, it's "all I need to support this body and life." Because of our world and the curse of sin that has infected it, our daily bread doesn't simply plop down in our laps. We have to earn it and then go get it, while fighting off everything that's trying constantly to take it away from us. Hard labor is one of the core values that parents try to impress on their children, wondering sometimes if they'll ever get the message! God could say, "Let there be . . ." and there it is. We, on the other hand, have to do something to put it there. So when we say that daily bread is given without our prayer, the first word that the selfish human nature is going to dispute is *given*. The objection is raised: What do you mean, *given*?

This is the big question asked around the table at Thanksgiving time, isn't it? I don't know what I'm thankful for, because I don't feel like I've been given anything. I rather feel like complaining about what I don't have! Gratefulness, contentment, generosity—these qualities are hard to come by when you look for them to bubble up by themselves from the human nature. Usually it takes a time of widespread difficulty, such as a disaster or poor economy, for people in general to adjust their priorities, get over thinking about what they don't have, and adopt a thankful spirit for the gifts they have been given.

James was clearly aware of this tendency in human nature. His reminder is for every time and place: (James 1:16–17) "Do not be deceived, my beloved brothers. Every good gift and every perfect gift is from above, coming down from the Father of lights with whom there is no variation or shadow due to change." Perhaps he had in mind that famous section from Ecclesiastes 3: "For everything there is a season, and a time for every matter under heaven: a time to be born, and a time to die." Apart from God's shining grace, the only constant thing we experience in this world is change itself. But even cynical-sounding Solomon, with all of his talk about "vanity" in the things of this world, still teaches us that there is true, God-given enjoyment in eating and drinking and pursuing the portion our Father provides us using the means of daily labor, or toil. Even though it may look to the untrained eye as though we achieve daily bread for ourselves, all of it comes from the gracious hand of God.

2 Also to All the Wicked (Matthew 5:45; Romans 4:5; 1 Timothy 2:4)

The best-selling book of the 1980s addressing the subject of theodicy was *When Bad Things Happen to Good People* by Rabbi Harold Kushner. However, the "elephant" in the room, that is, something everybody has on his mind but can't bring himself to ask, can be stated in the reverse question: "Why do good things happen to bad people?" It's the ultimate frustration that people eventually have with a theology of glory, the thinking that God should bless people who fully commit their lives to Him. Suffering shouldn't be the lot I get! I pray and read the Bible faithfully, I help others who are in need, I attend church. Then, as my eye wanders over to observe Hypocrite A and Unbeliever B, I can actually be driven away from the faith by their comparatively easy lives. If God isn't going to play fair, then I want nothing of Him, so declares the self-righteous heart.

Don't think you're alone in noticing this sun shining on both the wicked and the faithful. Keeping this frustration to yourself is not going to help you spiritually. Psalm 94 plainly lays out this complaint in the only God-pleasing way: in prayer to Him, accompanied with the earnest cry "How long?" (v. 3). The comfort from the perspective of the psalmist originates from the promise of a final vengeance, namely, the Lord's awaited retribution that will call His enemies to full account for their evil. One day, the evildoer will be wiped out, but till then, what's the Christian to do?

Our thoughts, prayers, and meditation on Scripture should turn our attention away from our almighty God's justice, because that is already decided and will come in due time. For now, we look to the merciful love of our heavenly Father. He is the one who justifies the wicked and makes believers out of His born enemies. While we were still sinners, Christ died for us. That in itself would have been enough, but even if it were just one more earthly blessing in addition to eternal salvation, that would be more than we should get. Radio and TV financial adviser Dave Ramsey answers his callers' question "How are you doing?" with this reply: "Better than I deserve." These words echo Paul's admission to Timothy, (1 Timothy 1:15) "Christ Jesus came into the world to save sinners, of whom I am the foremost." If our Savior is going to bestow His ultimate and greatest gift on the likes of sinners such as us, then we shouldn't be surprised if His lesser, earthly gifts were to be scattered about with just such reckless abandon. What matters most of all is our merciful Father's desire for all to come to the knowledge of the truth, and from that desire, we hear His command to pray for our enemies.

3 God Gives through Means (John 13:12–17; Matthew 25:34–40)

In Matthew 25, Jesus depicts Judgment Day as His dividing the people into two groups. Then He praises the one group for all the times they aided Him and condemns the other group for all the times they refused to help Him. On hearing these words, both groups stand dumbfounded! How could this be so? We didn't see You, Jesus . . . at least we didn't think we did. And as it turns out in this depiction of the last judgment, there will be quite a surprise in store for everyone. Jesus is telling us in this "little apocalypse" that opportunities to serve Him will abound throughout our lives, and we will often not know that they are there. "As you did it to one of the least of these" refers not to those who are considered least in the kingdom of heaven (see Matthew 5:19), but rather those who are esteemed least in the eyes of this world (5:1–12).

Christ identifies with the meek, those who are poor in spirit, and with the lowly, because He took on that very form when He came to earth. He did not come with demands for power, attention, and prestige. He came to serve in utter humility, so that He could properly be called the "least" among all members of the human race. At Christmas, we hail Him as Immanuel, not merely because He put on flesh, but also because He willingly adopted our sinful flesh. As true God and true man, Jesus Himself became the means of the Lord's reconciliation with mankind. He was, is, and always will be the Word of God. By Him, the heavens and the earth were made (Colossians 1:16), and at the time in earth's history when the Word became flesh (John 1:14), God brought Himself near, but not in His terrifying, judging glory. There will be a time and a place for that. But for now, the Gospel stands as a witness to our God with us, who came in the fullness of time and by means of His flesh achieved our salvation.

So from the trees in Eden to the burning bush to the horn blown by Joshua at Jericho to the great fish in the account of Jonah to the mud Jesus made by spitting on the ground, our Lord has demonstrated His delight in the use of means. Through ordinary things, God does His awesome work. The world may despise the Lord's doctrine, belittle Baptism, and complain about Communion, but these truly are precious gifts, and they should be at the top of the list of what makes daily bread. To be sure, Word and Sacrament are given us for the sake of our faith and to bring us to eternal life, yet they are still a necessity, also for this body and earthly life. The ear welcomes the Word (the eyes and hands do so with sign language), the skin gets wet with Baptism, and the mouth and tongue offer themselves to be the "cradle" for Jesus' body and blood, for He is the true bread of Bethlehem.

Then, from these great Means of Grace, we have our senses sharpened to notice all the other "means" by which God blesses us and proclaims life to us. We can hear all of creation singing praise to Him simply by existing and doing nothing that looks spectacular to the untrained eye. And in good times or in bad, there is a heightened awareness that all things indeed are working together precisely for our good, as our Lord operates in this life through the means of His creation.

4 Vocation: God's Instruments to Answer Prayer (1 Corinthians 12:27–13:13)

It is our bounteous God's good pleasure to work through means in this world, and an important aspect of this is the doctrine of vocation. From the word for "call," *vocation* reminds us of our particular stations in life. Because of God's blessings in Christ, we fulfill our Lord's holy calling in these stations. In a proper understanding of vocation, the true relationship between faith and good works is explained (Ephesians 2:8–10), and Christian prayer is given a helpful and valuable context.

Martin Luther emphasized vocation throughout his career. He was constantly fighting the idea of works-righteousness and seeking to defend the Gospel. According to the teaching of the time, one's ordinary calling and way of life was not good or holy enough. Now the saints, so it was held, had been even holier than they needed to be and so had earned extra merits. These merits of the saints were gifts that the Church hierarchy supposedly could dish out to those people who wished to appropriate this grace to themselves or for others. This became one of the factors that led Luther to post his Ninety-five Theses in 1517, offering to debate the sale of indulgences, a scheme that claimed to give out the stored-up merits of holy people to certain "unholy" people who had money they could give to the Church.

Later on in the history of the Reformation, works-righteousness reared its head again, but this time in the camp of the Protestants. Instead of arguing against indulgences and penitential requirements for earning God's grace, the Lutheran fathers fought against a strong legalistic desire to set up a pure, Christian kingdom, governed by the Old Testament Law of Moses, with its leaders imposing forms of discipline intending to attain perfection on earth in the present life. Just as before, the common person who believed in Christ for forgiveness and eternal life was simply not "awakened" enough. Such people were castigated for holding property, obeying secular government, serving in the military, and engaging in commerce with non-Christians. But the scriptural doctrine of vocation came to their rescue, comforting them with the assurance that their daily life was already pleasing to God because of what Christ had done for the whole world, not because they had submitted to any particular kind of rule.

Vocation is the God-given venue for good works that are pleasing to Him. It ensures that Christians know with confidence that it is God Himself doing the work through them. Ordinary Christians, as baptized priests of the Lord (1 Peter 2:9), become the very means He uses to answer their neighbors' prayers. Not just jobs are meant by "vocation"; your role as a mother, child, grandfather, sister, citizen, friend, motorist, or neighbor is also considered a holy calling. The works that to the casual observer seem plain and ordinary, even "unspiritual," are blessed works not because of what is done, but because the believer has saving faith in Jesus Christ. Good works, including prayer for self and for neighbor, proceed not from a stern requirement or promise of reward, but from a heart that God Himself has claimed, cleansed, and renewed.

5 Receive Our Daily Bread with Thanksgiving (Philippians 4:10–20; Colossians 3:17)

Daily bread is nourishment for our journey. As we eat the bread of life in faith and drink from the living water, our Lord abundantly provides all the rest that will sustain us in the body on our way. Food and drink, transportation, government, protection, neighbors, conveniences, and pastimes are only the beginning of the list. Paul reminds us, (Romans 8:32) "He who did not spare His own Son but gave Him up for us all, how will He not also with Him graciously give us all things?"

We do, however, still need to see the loving hand of God when He allows difficulty to come our way. That, too, is daily bread, and that's not as easy to take and still retain an attitude of thanksgiving. As the apostle Paul describes for the Philippians the highs and lows of his career, he traces the path of true contentment in the midst of it all. In a summary verse that has brought encouragement to many through the years, Paul reveals the Spirit-taught secret to facing plenty and hunger, abundance as well as need: (Philippians 4:13) "I can do all things through Him who strengthens me." He counsels Timothy with similar advice, especially for those times when some aspects of daily bread seem to be lacking: (1 Timothy 6:6–8) "Now there is great gain in godliness with contentment, for we brought nothing into the world, and we cannot take anything out of the world. But if we have food and clothing, with these we will be content." As someone once said, no one ever attaches a trailer full of possessions to a hearse!

Jesus Christ, along with His mercy shown to us in His life, death, and resurrection, is the true contentment that strengthens us. By virtue of our royal priesthood, we have been given all things. Our Lord promises that the meek, the ones who want all the best for others rather than for themselves, are the ones who will inherit the earth. It's not about doing something pleasing to God so that He will reward you with earthly blessings. It's rather about believing in His Son, who is the giver of every good and perfect gift as well as the one who bestows a giving nature in the hearts of the faithful. Do you truly want all the best of God's blessings that He has in store for you? Then make it your intention in the name of the Lord Jesus to give all that you can to others out of thankfulness, continually praying for them. Your Shepherd will assure you that neither you nor they will ever be in want.

Conclusion

Whenever we pray, we know that it is already done in Christ. This has been seen with all of the petitions that we have studied so far. It is also true when we pray for daily bread, the needs of our earthly life. We may sound like beggars as we approach our Father with our hand out, as it were, pleading for basic staples. Our human nature would rather take care of things by ourselves, but the proper perspective is that God has given us our skills and vocations as means to provide for us according to His grace. And because in our sinful world the good and the evil alike benefit from our Father's mercy, we are from that reality given the ability and opportunity to pray for our enemies as Jesus did. All that we receive comes from His hand, so that the Holy Spirit produces contentment and a thankful heart within us.

Concluding Activities

Conclude the session with an appropriate prayer and distribute the study leaflet for week 6.

Prayer's Reliance on Forgiveness

Selected Passages

Preparing for the Session

Central Focus

Forgiveness of sins is granted in Baptism, but it is also applied whenever the Christian hears the Word of Christ in the Gospel and receives forgiveness and strengthening of faith in the Lord's Supper. Thus forgiven, Christians confidently pray to their heavenly Father and are ready to forgive and pray for their neighbor.

Objectives

That participants, led by the Holy Spirit working through God's Word, will

1. make the connection between forgiveness, prayer, and the Christian life;
2. utilize the biblical principles of Law and Gospel in personal prayer; and
3. apply the power of forgiveness to their prayers for their needs and as they pray for others.

Note for the small-group leaders: Lesson notes and other materials you will need begin on page 71.

For the Lecture Leader

Session Plan

Worship

Begin the session with the hymn printed in the study leaflet. Accompaniments are available in denominational hymnals, such as *Lutheran Service Book* or *Lutheran Worship* (refer to hymnal index). (Note: Concordia Publishing House has available *The Concordia Organist.* All the initial worship hymns in the LifeLight courses are included in this resource. It's especially helpful for mission congregations and small parishes. See the list of study resources on p. 7.) Follow with this prayer:

Prayer

Merciful Lord, we know that our prayers would fail if it weren't for Your gracious forgiveness. Call us to repentance over our sins and comfort us with Your precious Gospel Word. Remind us that despite what we deserve as wandering sheep, You have abundantly provided us with every gift of body and soul, for you are pleased to be our Good Shepherd. Help us also to extend that free forgiveness also to those who hurt us with their sins. In Jesus' name we pray. Amen.

Lecture Presentation

1 Law and Gospel in Prayer (2 Timothy 2:15; 2 Peter 3:9)

The principle of distinguishing Law and Gospel is essential in understanding Scripture. It is "rightly handling [dividing] the word of truth" (2 Timothy 2:15). Knowing which statements from the Bible are Gospel promises and which are demands is a skill that helps us stick to the pattern of sound words whenever we speak about the Holy Trinity. But just as Law and Gospel are the tools we use to read and study God's Word, so also is it through the Law and Gospel that God's Word does His holy work on us.

The Holy Spirit uses the written Word of Scripture to create faith in our hearts. While it may be mysterious how a simple message can work such a magnificent conversion in a sinner, this work is certainly not done in a magical or unintelligible way. One needs to hear the Good News of Jesus, our Savior, in order to be saved, not merely read and recite a certain number of syllables. Certainly, a powerful feeling *may* accompany the wonderful gift of the forgiveness of sins, but trying to create that feeling in place of the substance of forgiveness makes as much sense as one trying to eat food simply by making a munching sound.

What's missing? There needs to be a transition from seeing the Bible *only* as a collection of life principles and historical information (and of course, parts of it certainly are those things) to seeing it as the powerful, salvation-bestowing Means of Grace that He has given His Church. Distinguishing Law and Gospel helps a person see that important transition. Our human reasoning has to give way when we consider that God's Word does what it says—it doesn't merely teach salvation, but it hands it out to the one who reads and hears it.

Some Christians say that anyone can pray certain words and invite Jesus to take over one's life and heart, an idea that is sometimes known as the "sinner's prayer." Actually, as we've been studying, prayer is a fruit and result of faith. It's one of the signs we have that Jesus is already inside our heart, already doing His good pleasure in our life. Baptism, not the act of praying a certain prayer, does God's powerful work of planting faith in the heart, and then that faith calls upon the Lord and speaks with love and thankfulness to our heavenly Father.

The letter of the Law kills us. Our sinful nature needs to be killed. Our sin lodges in our flesh and tries to take over our faith. We can read all we want about principles and commitments and commandments, but all we will ever find with God's Law is a mirror flashing back our own sinful ugliness. Even when the Law does its other tasks, like curbing gross outbreaks of sin or guiding Christians in living a Christlike life, it will always at the same time accuse us and point out our sin. If the Bible was meant to only tell us how to live, it would be comprised of only the Law, and our forgiveness would be a farce at best.

The Gospel gives life. We are raised up with Christ. The Bible does not merely inform us of salvation. It does not tell us that it is possible for a person to come to Jesus. That would be just as likely as a corpse springing to life and walking all on its own. The Word actually hands out Jesus and all His work to us. The Gospel is all forgiveness without condition. It is grace poured into our laps without waiting for us to do something with it. It is not some sort of spiritual raw material that we have to construct for ourselves into saving faith. The Gospel doesn't wait for us to pray; instead, it gives us the very faith in our hearts and words in our mouths so that we can truly pray. The Law may describe for us a godly life, but the Gospel breathes into us God's own life.

2 Praying for Forgiveness of All Sins (Psalm 51:1–12)

Sin is sin. The Law tells us without reservation that all sin is rebellion against God, who created us and gave us life. It includes the sin that we have inherited from Adam and that which we have added on our own. Keeping God's Law is not a matter of degrees or comparison to others, which is the way we like to look at laws. (Officer, there were lots of people speeding, some of them going much faster than I was!) The apostle James does not sugarcoat it: even if we could keep every law yet fail in only one point, we would still be guilty of breaking all of it. It's all or nothing.

To be sure, the various sins we commit can affect us and our faith in different ways. However, this distinction is found merely in the results and earthly consequences of each different sin, not in how it offends against God. Our sinful human nature can rationalize that because a certain action doesn't hurt anybody, it can't be all that bad. Plus, when decent, reasonable, outward human behavior can come from non-Christians as well as from Christians, the issue of sin can become easily confused. One could easily think that because someone appears to live a simple and honest life without ever doing anything intentionally wicked, that God has to make that count for something, especially in light of all the hypocritical Christians who seem to be out there.

David's psalm of confession reverses our human nature's need to make God fit into our sense of justice. The king who was praised as a man after God's own heart had to bring himself in sincere repentance to say to the Lord, (Psalm 51:4) "Against You, You only have I sinned." This was not a way for him to escape the guilt of hurting people; rather, it was an admission that every sin that is committed against another person is really a transgression against God Himself.

The Divine Service's general confession of sins (see *LSB*, p. 184) adds another dimension to how important forgiveness is to our prayer when it includes the phrase "with which I have ever offended You." Our sins have created an offense that is constantly tearing us away from our heavenly Father. We cannot claim to be unaware of sin and expect to be pardoned by reason of ignorance. The almighty Judge holds us responsible for that too. All of this is meant to drive us to Christ, for He is our only refuge. His ever-pleading sacrifice of holy, precious blood covers our ever-offending sins. Giving His last breath on the cross was what declared us "innocent from hidden faults" (Psalm 19:12). The confidence to pray is identical to the confidence in which we stand before God fully forgiven. What a blessing it is to be given the treasure of the Lord's Prayer, in which we may plead guilty of all sins, even those we are not aware of, and be comforted by the assurance that our Father will have mercy on us!

3 Private Absolution's Value to Prayer (John 20:19–23)

What is justification? In modern usage outside the Church, the word *justify* stands for someone's effort to make an action or thing seem right and necessary, sometimes even when it really shouldn't be considered as such. (The employer used the preliminary sales figures to justify his decision to fire the employee whom he secretly disliked.) Given this shady moral connotation, the concept of justification can become confusing if it is heard in the church setting without proper explanation.

As a doctrine, you may have realized that justification is the most important teaching that the Bible has given us, or as Lutherans have historically put it, the doctrine "on which the Church stands and falls." Because of the epic Reformation struggle over whether or not good works are necessary to merit salvation, our Lutheran fathers used the term "forensic justification" to be unmistakably precise. Forensics, of course, has to do with a legal decision, proclaimed by a judge, upon the gathering of appropriate evidence that has been considered in a case. The pronouncement of guilt or innocence is a binding decision and has long-lasting effects. Using the courtroom imagery, God, the almighty judge, considers the evidence of your sin over against the plea of your Advocate, Jesus Christ, who offers up His own blood to pay the full price for your guilt. The final decision for all time and into eternity in your case is *innocent*! By faith in Christ, although the Law says you are a sinner and you deserve eternal punishment, you are justified forensically, that is, forgiven by the Lord's declaring it to be so.

Jesus wanted you to hear that certain and unshakable pronouncement with your own ears, even before that final Judgment Day. That is why He breathed on His disciples, those who became the first called and ordained servants of the Word and said: (John 20:22–23) "Receive the Holy Spirit. If you forgive the sins of any, they are forgiven them; if you withhold forgiveness from any, it is withheld." They, and those who follow, are the Lord's own mouthpiece to declare His judgment. Of course, pastors do not make the decision for Him whether to forgive or not to forgive. Rather, in speaking the Absolution, they are announcing the forgiveness that has already been accomplished through Christ. So the concept of a forensic, declaratory justification emerges from a mere abstraction and takes form in a comforting, real forgiveness that is placed right inside the penitent sinner's ear.

What a burden that is then removed! Of course, Absolution loses its Gospel power if it is turned into a work, a requirement, or a torture that requires a penitent to confess every sin. If you hear the objection that Absolution is Roman Catholic, the response is easy: biblical Confession and Absolution is not just a matter of freedom; it actually gives forgiveness rather than merely prescribing actions that a person has to take to earn grace for oneself. By God's design, forgiveness comes in many forms, including when one reads the Bible, listens to the sermon in church, and partakes of the Lord's Supper. The forgiveness in one form is not a better forgiveness than what is provided in another form, nor are Christians given some legalistic demand to "touch every base" to be sure that they have all of their sins forgiven. No one should construe this into the outlandish claim that someone cannot be forgiven unless they go to a pastor. Private Confession and Absolution is best understood as a service that the pastor, in faithfulness to his divine call, can provide to his flock to proclaim the Gospel one-on-one, tailored to a particular person with a particular burden that needs to be lifted. It is not a replacement for the believer's praying for forgiveness. It is, in fact, the very answer to that prayer and a realization of our most important article of faith: justification.

4 Praying to Forgive Others (Matthew 18:21–35; James 5:16–20)

They are just eight simple words, but they can be hard to get out of my poor, injured, selfish heart: "As we forgive those who trespass against us." I can remember the offense too vividly to forgive it. It plays over and over again in my mind in some twisted version of meditation. I've looked in the Lord's Prayer for the words "as we *try to* forgive those," but to no avail. They aren't there. We are to pray knowing that even this part of the petition is a done deal.

This is probably the number-one area in which the more that we trust our experiences, the less we will rely on the promises of God's Word. This is the easiest speck to spot in someone else's eye and the most difficult plank to remove from our own. It's even worse when we end up hurt by a friend or close member of our family or someone we had implicitly and consistently trusted. When we suffer at the hands of a fellow Christian, the resulting anger can fester like gangrene and destroy a whole family or congregation, one abused soul at a time.

Our Lord spoke in wild extremes as He explained this to Peter and the rest of the disciples through the parable of the unmerciful servant (Matthew 18:21–35). In doing so, He drove home two main points: first, the contrasting debt amounts represent the infinite difference between our sins' offense against our Lord and the harm that our neighbor has committed against us. The second is His sincere threat of the severe punishment of separation from God if we should ever act as though forgiveness meant nothing to us and close it off from our neighbor. The first point gives us a better perspective to help us fight back our personal sense of indignation. The second one warns us that without the predominance of our Father's forgiveness in our way of life, our very faith will be in peril.

But even this is not handed down to us as an impossible demand, nor is the idea to be taken backwards, as if our forgiving others were the prior condition to our being forgiven. When I refuse to forgive someone, it's not like I'm breaking some sort of commandment, such as "thou shalt not be stingy with your forgiveness." Instead, it's a sign that I am stifling the very grace of God that has saved me. My own faith, the avenue by which I receive forgiveness, is getting blocked by my self-serving human nature. If I am holding a grudge, I must confess that sin, to be sure. But before I can resume my Christian vocation and willingly forgive those who trespass against me, I must first believe that I am freely and abundantly forgiven before the throne of my heavenly Father. No lecture on obedience will ever bring that out of my heart. Only the Gospel can work the miracle of forgiveness that the Lord has given me and every Christian the privilege to hand out.

5 Reconciliation before Sacrifice (Matthew 5:21–26; 18:15–20)

Who should make the first move? When one Christian sins against another, who is the one that Jesus says will begin the process of reconciliation? In Matthew 18, the well-known instructions from our Lord list as the first step, (v. 15) "Go and tell him his fault, between you and him alone." But in the Sermon on the Mount, beginning in Matthew 5, Jesus zeros in on the person who is able to perceive that he has offended another: If you "remember that your brother has something against you, . . . go. First be reconciled to your brother" (vv. 23–24).

While you may not be surprised to hear that the answer is "both," the unbelieving world is struck incredulous at the very thought. Outside the Lord's kingdom of grace, one's response is simply understood to strike back, to tear down an enemy, or at least to wait, with crossed arms and tapping foot, for the person to come crawling. A flood of examples may start filling your mind so that you become tempted to rationalize how Jesus' guides to reconciliation are simply not possible. What may have even started out as righteous anger can quickly change color into an evil and faith-killing rage.

Our Lord so highly prized reconciliation that He places it as a higher priority than the gift of sacrifice. Jesus said, "Leave your gift there before the altar" (v. 24), whether that would be a physical or spiritual thank offering. Even if it is a mere misunderstanding, it is more important to clear things up than to risk ascending the hill of the Lord with dirty hands.

Well, you may say, how can I go through life wondering if I've offended somebody? At that rate, I'd never end up worthy to approach the Lord! And the answer to that is *precisely*. Again, the Law says reconciliation is impossible to do on your own. It had to be done for you, accomplished by One who truly had clean hands and a pure heart. (James 5:16) "The prayer of a righteous person has great power," so remember that you have your Savior Jesus standing as Advocate before the heavenly tribunal, representing your case. Use Psalm 19 as your own prayer in this matter: (vv. 12–13) "Who can discern his errors? Declare me innocent from hidden faults. Keep back Your servant also from presumptuous sins; let them not have dominion over me!"

As you pray, don't be surprised if your heavenly Father should bring a matter to your attention where reconciliation is needed. His sound advice will ring in your ears, (Ephesians 4:26) "Do not let the sun go down on your anger." The same is true for your brother who has something against you. The devil will also be right there, trying at that moment to use it as leverage to drive a wedge. But as you pray, trust that you will receive a clear option and all the tools needed so that divine reconciliation becomes a reality.

Conclusion

Prayer relies on our Lord's merciful pardon that He grants us on account of Christ. The Law is needed to point out our dire spiritual situation and drive us to the message of the Gospel, which is centered on the cross. Absolution that we receive from our heavenly Father, and that we give to our neighbor in Jesus' name, is essential to the Church as a community of believers, for it is that word of Gospel forgiveness that sustains us, even to all eternity.

Concluding Activities

Conclude the session with an appropriate prayer and distribute the study leaflet for week 7.

Prayer's Battle against Our Enemies

Selected Passages

Preparing for the Session

Central Focus

The Christian's battle, in all of life as well as in prayer, is one of defense against real spiritual enemies. But we are not left defenseless. This lesson will lead participants to find God's protection from temptation and His gift of endurance during a time of trial.

Objectives

That participants, led by the Holy Spirit working through God's Word, will

1. revisit Old Testament narratives that describe the believer's battle against temptation;
2. locate God's deliverance in Baptism and the Lord's Supper; and
3. place Christ crucified at the center of their life and prayer.

Note for the small-group leaders: Lesson notes and other materials you will need begin on page 75.

For the Lecture Leader

Session Plan

Worship

Begin the session with the hymn printed in the study leaflet. Accompaniments are available in denominational hymnals, such as *Lutheran Service Book* or *Lutheran Worship* (refer to hymnal index). (Note: Concordia Publishing House has available *The Concordia Organist.* All the initial worship hymns in the LifeLight courses are included in this resource. It's especially helpful for mission congregations and small parishes. See the list of study resources on p. 7.) Follow with this prayer:

Prayer

Father, we thank You for granting us the armor that helps us in our fight against temptation. Bear us up in Your arms when the cross seems too heavy to bear. Help us as we strengthen one another so that Your love and mercy may have free course in Your Church now and until Christ comes again in glory, for it is in His name that we pray. Amen.

Lecture Presentation

1 How to Fight the Real Enemies (Ephesians 6:10–20)

Have you followed the TV sensation known as the ghost -hunting reality show? Several kinds of these programs have popped up and attracted millions of fans. Some of them have their experts creep around a darkened building with a suspenseful sound track that keeps the audience clinging to the edge of their seat. One hunting tactic they typically use involves one of the team trying to begin a conversation with a certain ghost, assuming that in some way a person who had lived or suffered a violent death at that place would answer, giving some sort of evidence that their sophisticated recording devices could pick up. This could either be an audible response or the movement of an object or a certain interaction with people or equipment. Other phenomena, such as unusual electromagnetic fields or a hot/cold zone as detected by an infrared camera, seem to point to something. But it's left up to interpretation, and that can vary greatly from show to show. Some are scientific and skeptical in their approach; others say that everything they record must prove that a location is haunted.

Much of the time, imaginations have certainly run wild in the name of entertainment. Other reasonable explanations for people's personal experiences always need to be explored. It could possibly be faulty wiring or plumbing rather than a spooky spirit. However, it remains true that our society's interest in a mysterious, unseen realm cannot pass by the Christian's notice without an opportunity to let God's Word speak to it. There is, of course, a lot that people want to know that Scripture simply doesn't tell. While God in His infinite power could conceivably grant an exception, the Bible assures us that souls of the faithful are safe with the Lord in paradise, awaiting the resurrection, while souls of unbelievers in torment are unable to go back to interact with those who have not yet died. Recall the parable of the rich man and Lazarus in Luke 16:19–31. If the rich man had received his wish, Lazarus would have been sent back "from beyond," as a Jacob Marley of sorts, to warn those five brothers who were destined for everlasting torment. Instead, the opposite lesson is clearly taught: spirits of people, no matter what had happened to them in this life, do not return to inhabit the earthly realm.

But that still doesn't answer the intriguing question of why people have such experiences and certain unexplained physical actions actually take place. Rather than shy away from this issue, we can speak with confidence on what God's Word does tell us about spirits, both good and evil, in our midst. Satan is our biggest, most consistent enemy. He is occupied with attacking our faith constantly, even though, as we have already studied, he and the evil spirits who were thrown down to the earth with him (Revelation 12:9) cannot make one move here among us without the Lord's permission. The sin-cursed world and our own flesh are in league with him, eager to believe his lies and oppose the truth. Angels serve the Lord and protect us from harm, both spiritual and physical. They are instruments of our Father's mercy toward us, His children. As the Nicene Creed says, God is the creator of "all things visible and invisible."

We may find ourselves contending against those who seem to us to be "flesh and blood," that is, other people. At those times, we need to be reminded that the battle is really against the unseen evil. It is real and formidable, yet we also need not fear that our God is stronger than all of it, and He will protect us. We should not test Him, assume wild theories in areas where Scripture is silent, nor take His armor for granted but rather acknowledge what we cannot see and strive for the preservation of our faith. With our Savior, that battle has already been won.

2 Fighting Temptation in the Old Testament (Genesis 16; 39; Exodus 32; Judges 16; 2 Samuel 11)

There are many names listed in the little historical treatise on faith that appears in Hebrews chapter 11. We should thank the Lord for this precious gem of Scripture that interprets Scripture. For without the emphasis on faith, we probably would have been duped into reading the Old Testament as though it had contained only moral examples to follow. Instead, as the Word of God itself tells us, this history that has been preserved in its pages has enabled us by the Holy Spirit to trace His gracious activity in the lives of His people.

The five Old Testament chapters we studied this week on the subject of temptation give us some well-known "heroes" of faith going through certain moments in their life that probably did not produce too many fond memories for them. We all have also likely gone through moments ourselves that we would rather not remember. The Holy Spirit did not give us Hebrews 11 in order to tell us that we go through our trials and temptations as a punishment for lack of faith. That would be inconsistent with the theology of the cross, as it is applied to our own lives. These saints of old did not soar above the everyday struggles of life—they were attacked in basic human matters too. Fleshly desires assailed them; even when they resisted them (Joseph refused sinful advances), they still faced great difficulty. Nevertheless, God's gift of faith gave them the final victory, as He promises also for us.

This faith is not isolated, and it is not centered in itself. God-given faith is placed in Christ and all that He has done for you. If one's faith is in anything else, it is a false faith. It is a faith placed not in God but rather in an idol. At some point during times of trial, the object of such a false faith will end up failing to provide lasting comfort for that person. Money will run out. Friends will desert. Family will disappoint. Fame will fizzle. As the hymn sings, when other helpers fail and comforts flee, only the true God will abide with us, and faith in Him will gain strength through tribulation.

When Jesus is found in His proper place, at the center of Scripture's accounts of faith, He is portrayed as Savior more than as a moral exemplar. In this way, the Bible is used not as a book of impossible rules but as a book of faith. The saints are offered up as our examples. This is not so that we would perform certain works like theirs as if to achieve God's blessings apart from Christ and definitely not so that we would petition them for help rather than the Lord. Instead, their lives recorded on the sacred page encourage us to keep clinging to Jesus. Our Father's promise, which had armed and strengthened the faithful of old during their times of struggle, will be there for us too.

3 Baptism and the Lord's Supper Strengthen Me (Galatians 3:27; John 6:54–65)

One of the pastor's tasks is to teach his flock to pray. When he hears a congregation member speaking about the power of prayer, no doubt he would rejoice. Any time a Christian turns in faith to our heavenly Father in a time of trial, it is good, right, and salutary. What causes concern for a pastor is when he hears prayer being characterized as though it is one's only source of God's blessing. Like with other signs or fruits of faith, man's tendency with prayer is to place confidence in it as a work. When times are tough, the Christian needs help that comes from the outside. The problem is, in spite of this, our human nature fools us into looking for it to come from inside of us, where there is nothing but sin and doubt.

Our Father knows our needs and how to address them better than we do. He doesn't make us guess when it comes to His grace. He encourages us to remember our Baptism, to recall that at a certain moment in our life, God brought His eternal salvation into our earthly existence, washed away all our sins, and renewed us to be filled with faith toward Him and love toward our neighbor. Do you need to know a particular time when you made the first move and decided to let Jesus come into your heart? Not with Baptism! As the Bible teaches it, your Baptism is the Lord's work as He comes to you before you could ever do anything for Him. He claims you through this salutary water for His kingdom. Because many Christians transform Baptism from a divine, Gospel act into a human, Law-oriented duty, they render themselves unable to see the power in it.

The same can be said of the Lord's Supper. If all that the bread and wine do is "represent" Christ's body and blood, then that makes the believer have to do something to achieve a connection of unity with God. Another error is just as bad: to turn the Lord's Supper into a sacrifice of Jesus that is offered up in the hope of earning grace. Holy Communion has also at times been reduced to be nothing more than an expression of some vague feeling of mutual love and acceptance rather than a group proclamation of true unity in the whole teaching of the faith. Again, an unhealthy trust in human works sifts the Gospel away from the Sacrament, and it loses its comfort. If we fall to this temptation, then faith falters and our connection with God could waver. When these gifts are stripped of their divine power and regarded as only symbols, prayer is sometimes called upon to pick up the slack and stand in for the Sacraments. That is something our Father never created it to do. In the absence of the Means of Grace as Scripture has instituted them, some Christians try to make prayer into a means of gaining favor from our Lord.

Instead, we need to remember that prayer, Baptism, and the Lord's Supper are not at odds with one another, but they work together. The Lord answers prayer through means, and that starts with Word, water, bread, and wine. When we pray, we don't wistfully reach out for our Lord; we take comfort that He has already taken hold of us. We don't try to demonstrate our love for God; we rejoice in what Jesus Christ has already done in love for us. We hold on to the physical, yet also divine, things that sign, seal, and guarantee that grace to us. Those things are the Word of the Gospel, our Baptism, and the blessed meal of our Lord's body and blood.

4 More Than I Can Bear? (Hebrews 12:3–13; 2 Peter 2:4–9)

Martin Luther had a famous saying that a theologian is made through three things: prayer, meditation, and spiritual trials, or as they are given in Latin: *oratio, meditatio, tentatio* (ten-TAH-tsee-o). Theologians who undergo these activities include not only the professionals who preach and teach the Word, but also the laypeople who pray, read, and suffer for that Word in their lives every day. Every Christian is being formed into a theologian. Prayer and meditation may be the two activities that easily make sense. But it's that third part, the struggle or *tentatio*, that can make this formation process difficult for us to understand.

What exactly is it about hardship that makes one stronger? How can it build me up, when it feels as though I'm being torn down? Remember, James had counseled his flock to be joyful when trials arise, because they produce steadfastness (1:2). But we sometimes find ourselves afraid that those same difficult trials could have just as easily shaken our faith and that in our despair, we would have been driven away from the Lord. Then who would be rejoicing?

To address this concern, Hebrews places our struggles within the framework of discipline. Not discipline as in a punishment for doing something wrong or God getting angry at us, but discipline as in teaching, a course of training and exercise of our faith that is tailor-made by the hand of a loving Father. (Hebrews 12:7) "God is treating you as sons" means more to us than the parent's line of, "I'm doing this because I love you." We are being reminded during times of trial that we belong to the Lord's kingdom and not to the world's, even though the experience that teaches us this truth can be unpleasant at the time. He disciplines us for our good, both temporal and eternal. Nothing merely "seems" best to God. That's the impression that fallible, human parents will get when they apply discipline to their children. Our heavenly Father, on the other hand, always knows perfectly that which is for our good.

His holy work is to transform us through trial into His holy people. At the same time, thanks to the sacrifice of Christ, we are already fully righteous in His sight, because our Father has declared it so by His grace. We have not resisted temptation to the point of shedding our own blood, but even if we must, we have the precious blood of Jesus to bear us up. The Lord knows how to rescue the godly from trials, and you know this with great confidence because you know that He raised Jesus from the dead. If you don't think that you are godly enough and therefore won't be rescued, look to the Scriptures and meditate on them. Repeat them to yourself; learn and use them as you pray. They will say unequivocally that you have been justified by grace as a gift. Look also to your Baptism, which most certainly has saved you. Struggles and crosses, which constitute that third *tentatio* step in your lifelong formation into a theologian, will continue to motivate you to pray. In answer to that prayer, God will grant you the patience to overcome them and claim Christ's victory.

5 Christ the Way of Escape (1 Corinthians 10:9–13)

Steven Slater was a flight attendant who suddenly decided that after a long, rough week, he needed to escape. While on the ground after a landing, he had requested a person who had stood up too early to please take a seat. When rebuffed, he apparently snapped into a tirade that included a thorough chewing-out of the entire load of passengers, a quick grab of some available alcohol, the opening of an emergency exit door of the plane, the deployment of the inflatable slide, and his escape onto the runway and off the airport property. It was a stunt that couldn't have been orchestrated better by the greatest Hollywood director. But the man didn't stay out of reach for long; authorities quickly surrounded his house nearby and eventually arrested him.

The world, especially as reported about on TV, radio, and the Internet, regarded Mr. Slater as a hero, even if his fame was short-lived. He was brave enough to speak his mind, and he went out with flair, giving no thought to the consequences. But he still failed to escape! He may have stood for everyone who had ever been fed up with a job and with life in general, but the escape certainly wasn't a lasting one for him.

When, during our times of testing and temptation, we may long for something like an exit door and a slide to get us out of all the mess that we face. However, we have the greater escape—not a way to avoid the difficulty, but rather the unfailing power to endure through it. That way of escape is our Lord Jesus Christ, who faced every kind of temptation, both those common to man and those that could easily have overpowered man. God is faithful because Jesus faithfully endured all struggles by way of the cross. All the sins of the world and the entire curse of God's judgment were dumped on His shoulders. He did not blast others, steal booze, or speak His mind in a flashy tantrum, but He received punishment quietly and willingly for your sake. His resurrection "slides" you, if you will, most assuredly into the Father's waiting arms, where your promised escape from sins and their cursed effects will at long last be permanent.

Conclusion

Temptation does not come from God, although He does allow it to enter our lives. The three enemies who attack us end up becoming His instruments of testing and strengthening. We then turn to our Lord in prayer and we meditate on His Word, confident of His protection and final deliverance. When we remember our Baptism, hear the Word of Absolution, and partake of the Lord's Supper, we experience our gracious God giving us the grace that we need to withstand and overcome.

Concluding Activities

Conclude the session with an appropriate prayer and distribute the study leaflet for week 8.

Prayer's Final Goal

Selected Passages

Preparing for the Session

Central Focus

Evil (and the evil one, Satan) desires us as its captive. Our journey through this world's valley of sorrow will, in God's own time, come to its blessed end, and our prayers today, in the midst of all of the short-term matters on our minds, should still reflect that big-picture perspective. Special emphasis will be given to the Bible's references to the believer's conscience.

Objectives

That participants, led by the Holy Spirit working through God's Word, will

1. trace the description of the conscience, especially in the New Testament epistles;
2. discover how the heavenly Father bestows a clear conscience on His children; and
3. look to the Lord's deliverance from evil in this world, and forward to our blessed end.

Note for the small-group leaders: Lesson notes and other materials you will need begin on page 79.

For the Lecture Leader

Session Plan

Worship

Begin the session with the hymn printed in the study leaflet. Accompaniments are available in denominational hymnals, such as *Lutheran Service Book* or *Lutheran Worship* (refer to hymnal index). (Note: Concordia Publishing House has available *The Concordia Organist*. All the initial worship hymns in the LifeLight courses are included in this resource. It's especially helpful for mission congregations and small parishes. See the list of study resources on p. 7.) Follow with this prayer:

Prayer

O Lord, our almighty God, we need Your protection. The evil one prowls around us like a roaring lion, seeking to devour Your children. Yet You, in great love for our souls, have promised that not one of us will be snatched from Your most powerful hand. Strengthen us in the times when we suffer evil in various forms, and bring us at last to our blessed end at home with You in heaven, in Jesus' name. Amen.

Lecture Presentation

1 Conscience, the Personal Battleground (Romans 15:30; 1 Corinthians 8:7)

Pinocchio received this timeless advice: "Let your conscience be your guide." Phrases like this lead us to think of conscience only in moral terms—as some voice inside telling us what we should or should not do. Our natural knowledge of right and wrong is described in Romans 2:15: "the law is written on their hearts." This guides us in our day-to-day decisions, even though this sense is now warped by the effects of sin and our own self-serving nature. Because it governs our outward actions, natural knowledge contributes greatly to the existence of civil righteousness, though it has no ability to have a direct effect on faith. If we were to limit conscience only to this inner moral compunction, then believers would have no distinct difference in conscience from unbelievers. Faith in Christ would then be unnecessary because works would become the only factor. Absolute truth would disintegrate into endless relativism: whatever is right for you may not be right for me, and so forth.

When the Bible speaks of our conscience, however, there is more going on than listening to whispered directions of "do this; don't do that." As you dig a little deeper, you find that its main idea is rooted in who you are, and what you do proceeds as a result of that. Think of the sheep and goats scene in Matthew 25: works are definitely mentioned in this picture of the last judgment. But the works do not make sheep into goats, nor do they transform the goats into sheep. Because of faith and unbelief, sheep are already sheep and goats are already goats by the time the final day comes. Conscience is your God-given awareness of who you are in God's sight. It's more than whether you "feel" like you're a Christian; it's a question of to what extent our Lord's forgiveness and the renewal of the Holy Spirit have permeated your being.

The world's best approximation of conscience in this full sense of the term is perhaps its concept of "self-esteem." In the world's wisdom, a good self-image seems to be achieved by having an upbeat attitude, being tolerant of others' differences, and learning to love yourself. All of this is a laudable goal of secular society, but we should also be honest in acknowledging its shortcomings in the spiritual realm. Because of its exclusively self-centered focus, the idea of promoting self-esteem will never comfort a person concerning his or her blessed standing in the sight of the Lord. Without faith in Christ and the fear of God as defined by the first Commandment, one's conscience will remain pagan, exclusively self-centered and opposed to what our heavenly Father has intended for mankind.

Conscience in the Christian is something that changes and progresses; it becomes soiled and hurt and purified again, not because God has done an incomplete job, but because the believer constantly faces various struggles. Luther said, "Sin pollutes the conscience," referring both to one's own wrongs as well as the wrongs done to him because both kinds of sin can do damage to faith. Satan attacks conscience whenever he introduces doubt of the Lord's mercy so that the child of God is led to think that He doesn't care.

Even the appearance of sin can wound the conscience. Those who are recent converts or who are still unaware of the blessings of full forgiveness and Gospel freedom are described in the New Testament as those whose faith is weak, and their conscience is fragile. Peter and Paul both had situations in which preserving the consciences of weak Christians was of utmost importance to them, which dictated how they responded. By taking care of each individual's conscience, they worked to repel evil in the lives of their flock.

2 The Gift of a Clear Conscience (Hebrews 9:11–14; 1 Peter 3:21)

Blood was everywhere in the temple! After a number of animal sacrifices would take place on a given day, according to the ceremonial laws of the Old Testament, little red rivers would stream across the stone floors. The smell, even when mingled with strong incense, would have repelled most of us today. The temple routine of the Hebrew would be thoroughly governed by an acute awareness of how and when he might become unclean followed by what he needed to do to get clean again. God called His people to be holy, and their ceremonial sanctification was vivid, unforgettable, and certainly not optional.

Take note of what Jesus said, as recorded in the Gospels, when He was at the temple in Jerusalem. In all likelihood, these animal sacrifices may well have been taking place in the background while the Lamb of God Himself was engaged in His teaching! People would have had their uncleanness on their mind, perhaps even with their unblemished animal standing there with them, and in the meantime the promised Messiah was telling them, "Look to Me to be made holy! I'm the one who will purify you!" Hebrews 9 recalls centuries of the "blood of goats and bulls," saying that if this can "sanctify for the purification of the flesh, how much more will the blood of Christ, who through the eternal Spirit offered Himself without blemish to God, purify our conscience" (Hebrews 9:13–14). The performance of sacrifices and ceremonies has come to an end, but the need for purity still endures. And as long as that need is there, we have our Savior as its only answer and fulfillment.

Paul announced to the congregation in Corinth that Christ is our sanctification. Because faith in Him is given to us as a pure gift, we do not go through a process to make ourselves holy to the Lord, whether that process is an Old Testament sacrificial ritual or a modern-day anguishing spiritual exercise. Our Baptism, St. Peter reminds us, works as "an appeal to God for a good conscience" (1 Peter 3:21; note that the NIV does not provide the best translation of this particular verse). Because our sins are paid for with the blood of Christ and because our gracious God has promised to save us through the waters of Holy Baptism, our conscience, our standing before the Lord, is affected not by the condemning Law, but by the forgiving and life-giving Gospel. Jesus purified us and made us clean forever! We have a lot in our world that makes us feel spiritually unclean. We have made our share of mistakes; others have hurt us very deeply. What we have been given is true purity from all of this spiritual pollution, and this is brought to our constant attention today not by temple rituals and slain animals, but by Baptism, Absolution, the Word, and the Sacrament of the Altar—in other words, the real things that give us Christ. By these physical, concrete gifts, we will be preserved sound and blameless until the return of our Lord. No matter how hard our struggle may get in this life, our conscience is clear—we know for certain where we stand with God.

3 Body and Soul, Possessions and Reputation (Titus 2:11–15; 1 Timothy 6:6–12)

When the Christian takes hold of the eternal life to which he or she is called, evil is ready to pounce with attacks aimed squarely on the present life. Our spiritual enemy knows where our human nature "itches" and also what will steal our attention from our heavenly Father. One hour a week in church can set our minds on things above, but all the rest of those hours clamor for our attention down here below. Everything of this world, from necessities down to conveniences, was put in its place when our Savior broke into this world, took our sins away, and then said, "I go to prepare a place for you."

One worldly thing that comes to us as a precious gift of God but that we often take for granted is our good name. As popular wisdom says, it takes a lifetime to build a reputation, and only a few moments to tear it down. The crime of identity theft runs rampant now. While of course its financial element is the most obvious concern, this kind of stealing hurts more than the pocketbook. Evils that violate the Eighth Commandment can linger longer than those of moth and rust.

Money is a lifeless representation of worldly value and energy spent in work, but you would think it had a life of its own. It seems to have the power to break up marriages, rend relationships, alienate family members, tear apart congregations, magnify the best and worst in people, and certainly keep the legal profession in business. Of course, you know from Paul's letter to Timothy that it is the *love* of money, rather than money itself, that is the root of all kinds of evil.

The sinful nature doesn't need to be taught the love of wealth; people want more and more right from the very beginning. Every avenue to acquire "stuff" will be explored, even godliness, if one should feel that there's a good chance to benefit from it. When efforts to satiate the love of money and possessions become thwarted, drastic measures begin to be employed. Due to the selfish flesh, the evil lust for "unrighteous wealth" (Luke 16:11) inflates, so that the true riches, the treasure in heaven, are forfeited.

On the contrary, it is contentment that needs to be taught, and what a difficult lesson that can be! Usually the lesson is taught through deprivation. Now, the world can learn by experience that one doesn't appreciate something until the moment one loses it. What is additional wisdom for the Christian's benefit is that these very teachable moments bring us to our knees so that we pray as our Father has encouraged us all along. (Psalm 50:15) "Call upon Me in the day of trouble." He promises that He will deliver you from that evil—maybe not by granting you a fortune, perhaps not by stopping your ridicule, and probably not by assuring that you will always be the perfect picture of health—but you will be delivered all the same, because "there is great gain in godliness with contentment" (1 Timothy 6:6). We are, even today, engaged in the act of leaving this world and its stuff, concerns, values, and worries all behind!

4 This Valley of Sorrow (Psalm 23; Revelation 7:13–17)

Driving through the Ozarks of southern Missouri makes you very familiar with hills. These aren't impressive mountain ranges that dominate the horizon ahead of you. Your car does not spend the bulk of its time and fuel scaling and switching back to get to a singular summit. No, it's more of a repetitive up-and-down and only a little bit of meandering here and there. You arrive at the top of one hill and the next top is usually right ahead of you in your sight line. Morning and evening, when the sun is low in the sky, those crests are the only islands in the whole vista laid out before you that are bathed in light.

Wouldn't it be nice if the car would hop from hill to hill, never leaving the sunlit spots? It would certainly make for a shorter trip, but that is just a vain daydream. There are valleys to go through as you drive those hills. The shadows, and perhaps a little fog in those places laced with water, hide from your view for a while whatever terrain you must negotiate before you ascend to the next bright spot on the road. This is the image that pops into mind when we consider "the valley of the shadow of death."

This illustration can be used to describe the progression of seasons in the Church Year from Transfiguration to Lent to Holy Week and finally to Easter. Jesus allowed a few of His disciples to catch a glimpse of His heavenly glory while they were on top of a mountain. Moses and Elijah appeared, speaking of His exodus in Jerusalem, namely, His death, resurrection, and ascension. With this rare view of bright splendor shining in his overwhelmed eyes, Peter offered to camp out so that the moment would last a bit longer.

Likewise, we want our "mountaintop" experiences of our Lord's majesty and wonderful works for us to continue unabated. We can see the future glory waiting, although it is still off in the distance. Easter is the next time when radiant glory will shine in our faces, but there's a season standing in between. With a sudden descent, almost straight down into the depths, we enter Lent with the severe, somber observance of Ash Wednesday. Lent winds us through darkness, sin, and the Law's just condemnation directed toward us. We are reminded of our mortality, which is the whole point of the valley of sorrow. The roughest, most intense part of this season of repentance is the steep, arduous climb at the end: Holy Week. Anticipating the sun of resurrection glory, we aren't sure if Good Friday will get us there. But it does.

This Easter goal for the Christian's life journey is pictured in the blessed scene from Revelation 7. All the "negatives," as it were, of heaven—no crying, no mourning, no pain—await us. By God's grace, we'll reach that final summit. The road ahead is dark and sometimes our Lord's wisdom will be hidden to us in this vale of tears, but "soon, soon to faithful warriors cometh rest" (*LSB* 677:6).

5 The Heavenly Goal, a Blessed End (2 Timothy 4:18)

While praying the liturgical prayer known as the Litany (see *LSB* pp. 288–89), I have often wondered why, centuries ago, Christians were taught to pray for the Lord's mercy to deliver them "from sudden and evil death." Isn't all death a manifestation of sin and evil? What is so undesirable about its possible suddenness that we should pray against it? I've typically heard: "When I go, I want to go quickly." One would think that, in a comparison, the evil death would not be the sudden one, but the one accompanied by a long, painful process, dragged out until the bitter end.

To be sure, whether people die quickly or slowly matters not for the issue of whether they have eternal life, for that was already decided by Jesus Christ on the cross and handed to each believer through the waters of Holy Baptism. No matter how it comes to the individual believer, death is still swallowed up in victory. The reason why a certain period of time is a blessing to the dying Christian is not in any improvement that it can bring to salvation (for no improvement is needed to Christ's work). Rather, it lies in the opportunities our Father provides the believer to pray, to grow a firm faith in the midst of adversity, and to allow friends and loved ones to show love and care.

A sudden death can be as innocuous as dying in one's sleep or as troublesome and full of difficult questions as in the case of a violent accident, murder, or suicide. In various ways, these short-circuit some of the above blessings. Again, that should not imply that the person will not go to heaven, which is a matter that is known for certain only to God, but the blessed end is still the one preferred. That is the end for which we pray each day, "Deliver us from evil," that is, let us use every chance You give us to trust in You, Lord, for our rescue.

Now, rather than fix our attention on the circumstances of our death, we should look beyond the conquered enemy to its Conqueror. Hebrews opens our eyes of faith to the great multitude of faithful saints surrounding us. We are in the midst of running a race, and we have those who have already finished it letting loose a roar of encouragement for us. We don't turn aside to the right or to the left in this lap. When our spiritual enemies try to cut in, we call on the Lord's help in order to hurdle those obstacles. Most important, we run the race "looking to Jesus, the founder and perfecter of our faith" (Hebrews 12:2). The finish line of death will take care of itself with our gracious heavenly Father holding us in the palm of His hand every step of the way. A blessed death is assured us in every way that it was assured to Paul: (2 Timothy 4:18) "The Lord will rescue me from every evil deed and bring me safely into His heavenly kingdom. To Him be the glory forever and ever. Amen."

Conclusion

Deliverance from evil in this life is provided in Christ's gift of a clear conscience. Evil attacks us in many ways, using many means, but the Lord provides us the perspective of eternal life and our ultimate home with Him in heaven.

Concluding Activities

Conclude the session with an appropriate prayer, and distribute the study leaflet for week 9.

Amen: The Last Word?

Selected Passages

Preparing for the Session

Central Focus

Every "amen" accentuates the confidence and divine gift that prayer is. To conclude our study, this lesson traces the use of the word in the Bible, including when Jesus says, "Amen, Amen" (ESV: "Truly, truly"). Students will be encouraged to extend prayer into a pattern of a uniquely Christian life lived in true and confident faith.

Objectives

That participants, led by the Holy Spirit working through God's Word, will

1. find out how the word *amen* is used in the Bible;
2. learn how both requests and thanksgivings work together in prayer; and
3. build a life of prayer that goes above and beyond mere words.

Note for the small-group leaders: Lesson notes and other materials you will need begin on page 83.

For the Lecture Leader

Session Plan

Worship

Begin the session with the hymn printed in the study leaflet. Accompaniments are available in denominational hymnals, such as *Lutheran Service Book* or *Lutheran Worship* (refer to hymnal index). (Note: Concordia Publishing House has available *The Concordia Organist*. All the initial worship hymns in the LifeLight courses are included in this resource. It's especially helpful for mission congregations and small parishes. See the list of study resources on p. 7.) Follow with this prayer:

Prayer

Heavenly Father, You have given us a precious gift in prayer. We thank and praise You for the confident "Amen" that takes a firm hold on all Your blessings. Grant that all doubt may be removed from our hearts, and bestow on us Your Holy Spirit in rich measure so that one day we will see the fullness of Your glory, at the return of Christ, our Lord. Amen.

Lecture Presentation

1 Old Testament Use of Amen (1 Chronicles 16:35–36; Habakkuk 2:4)

You almost say it without thinking. It's simply the ending to a prayer. Even when someone else is actually speaking the prayer, it is understood that you may speak an "Amen" when the prayer comes to a close. It may even be expected, to be considered the same as if you had offered that prayer yourself. Parents have trained their children well to say "Amen." Even though those inquisitive questions from young minds never seem to have a limit, it still may take several years before a child asks, "Why do we say 'Amen'?"

"Amen" is basically identical in every language because it is an untranslated Hebrew word. Linguists will tell you that it doesn't seem to have been borrowed from another language. It is constructed, like the great majority of native Hebrew words, out of a root of three consonants. (Strictly speaking, written Hebrew doesn't have vowels; the proper pronunciation is approximated by a system of vowel points.) Those consonants are Aleph, Mem, and Nun. There's no equivalent to Aleph in English, so it is represented by an apostrophe when you see it in the notes of most study Bibles. Its sound is an almost imperceptible "catch" in your throat that you might feel just before you start saying a word such as "and" or "egg." Mem and Nun are like the letters *M* and *N*. The root word *'aman* and the related noun *'emunah* mean "firmness, truth, faithfulness." When "Amen" is spoken in the Old Testament, it is used especially in psalms, in other worship contexts, and in solemn oaths to communicate the basic idea, "This is firm; I know this to be true."

Deuteronomy 27 listed several solemn curses against certain sins, some of them particularly heinous. When the people listening to the curse assented by saying "Amen," they also in effect pronounced that curse on themselves if they went on to disobey God (see *TLSB* text note, p. 319). What is true for curses is especially so also for blessings, as in Psalm 106:48, where petitions for the Lord's salvation, together with the blessings pronounced upon His name, are accompanied with the response of the people, "Amen!"

Words in the Old Testament describing God's faithfulness are related to "Amen." Among the most prominent of these quoted in the New Testament is Habakkuk 2:4, "The righteous shall live by his faith." The Lord's faithfulness to the believer creates the saving faith in his heart that gives him life. That is an "Amen," so to speak: a firm, reliable truth straight from God that will never be overturned or taken away. In Deuteronomy 7, the Lord describes Himself as "the faithful God who keeps covenant and steadfast love." The word "faithful" is actually a participle built from the "Amen" root word. You might think about it this way: God "Amens" Himself toward us, that is, He gives to us His firm and truthful assurance that He will remain faithful to His saving promises. He will make sure about it, even to the point of swearing an oath by Himself to confirm it. As Hebrews 6 teaches us, God cannot swear by anything or anyone greater than He is, so He calls Himself to witness on His own promises, and it is impossible for God to lie. To that we can say a confident "Amen!"

2 Jesus' "Amen" Statements (John 16:20–24)

Jesus Christ is the faithful one; the Book of Revelation (3:14) even calls Him the "Amen." So when our Savior uses the word "Amen" while He is proclaiming His Word in the Gospels, He is affirming that absolute faithfulness and solid truth that He is for us. He has a generous helping of that "Amen" to lavish upon us for our eternal benefit. Almost always, when Jesus says "Amen," it is at the very beginning of a very important word of truth. He makes sure that the disciples are paying close attention with a phrase that He then repeats: "Amen, I say to you." In English, the "Amen" is usually translated as "truly" or "verily." And He says it often! In Matthew, there are thirty-one verses including this phrase; Mark has it fourteen times, while Luke has seven verses with those words. Exclusively in the Gospel of John, we find Jesus employing the unique double "Amen," so our translations usually render it, "Truly, truly I say to you" (and that occurs in a total of twenty-four verses). But these opening words are much more than an attention-getting device. With the statements that Jesus leads off with an "Amen," He indicates that He is eager to plant true faith in the hearts of His hearers.

Throughout His preaching and miracle-working ministry, Jesus is relentlessly searching, hunting for faith. When He finds it even stronger in Gentiles, He is amazed at their great faith. When the Canaanite woman, whom He had earlier rebuffed as a dog, responds, "Yet even the dogs eat the crumbs from the masters' table," then Christ says, "Great is your faith!" (Matthew 15:21–28). He knows His handiwork when He sees it! His "Amen" word of sure promise, His guarantee that He came to save the lost, wins out, even when it seems to us through our experiences that He is refusing us.

When Jesus says "Amen," it is a signal to you who hear Him speaking to you today in the preaching of His Word that what He is about to do or say in the rest of that Gospel passage is a matter of your eternal life with Him. You can think of the phrase "Amen, [or Truly,] I say to you" as your Lord's solemn oath that He truly has done everything out of steadfast faithfulness to you as His precious child. All that He suffered was for the strengthening of your faith. And when He comes again on the Last Day, He will find faith on the earth. According to His own "Amen" promise, He has placed faith by means of His Word in your heart, and the Word of God will not return to Him empty.

3 "This Gift Is Also for Me" (Mark 11:20–25; 1 John 5:13–15)

At the beginning of our study on prayer, we highlighted the confidence that God gives to His baptized people who pray. Now, as we have been studying the word "Amen," we can tie this unique, biblical word together with that confidence of faith. Martin Luther has already instructed us in the Small Catechism that "Amen, Amen" means "Yes, yes, it shall be so." Anyone who prays should have some form of assurance that the thing prayed for will come about. But when we consider the constant onslaught of doubt and other spiritual enemies, this confident "Amen" from our human lips becomes anything but automatic.

We have commonly heard the word "Amen" as an expression of agreement or heartfelt, positive emotion. Sometimes it is belted out spontaneously with great fer vor! The Lutheran liturgy also employs "Amen" and sets it aside almost exclusively for the congregation. In fact, in the Divine Service settings in *Lutheran Service Book* (pp. 151–218) the pastor speaks or sings this important term only when he is joining in with the congregation, such as when the *Nunc Dimittis* is sung (see p. 165), when the Creed is confessed, and when the Lord's Prayer is prayed.

The use of the word "Amen" in the distribution of the body and blood of Christ in the Holy Communion helps bring to light another important aspect that it expresses in addition to agreement. On page 199, the pastor and assistants say, "Take, eat," and those who receive may respond, "Amen." It's in bold print so that it is clear that it is meant as a response. We say "Amen" to agree with our Lord Christ that His true body and blood are hidden in the earthly elements and also to say, "Yes, Lord! I believe that you have set aside this precious gift even for me." This expanded meaning of "Amen" isn't merely an emotional outburst whose effect will soon wear out. It can be our confident and faithful assent whenever we receive any blessing from the Lord, whether we hear it from Scripture, say it in our prayers, or have it placed into our own mouths.

George F. Handel's *Messiah* oratorio may be best known for its "Hallelujah" chorus, but in its full version, this master work closes with a magnificent finale taken from the Book of Revelation. Following the text "Worthy is the Lamb that was slain," there is a choral fugue that contains nothing else but the word "Amen" repeated over and over. Even though the idea is most likely from Revelation 5:14, I like to think of this multiple "Amen" as a final affirmation of all the previously quoted Scriptures in the oratorio that had predicted and described the life and work of Jesus, the Messiah.

When the oratorio proclaimed Isaiah's words, "Surely, He hath borne our griefs," the "Amen" that is sung at the end of the work can be taken to mean that our Lord did that even for me. When it echoes the words of Psalm 69:20, "Thy rebuke hath broken His heart," we can be confident that through Christ, God's rightful rebuke is turned away from us forever. Amen! As you can see, for the Christian, "Amen" is more than just the ending of a prayer; it's our most basic statement of faith in our Lord and our acknowledgement that His gifts indeed have been received. Hallelujah!

4 With Thanksgiving Let Your Requests Be Made Known to God (Colossians 4:2; Philippians 4:4–7)

"The Lord is at hand," Paul writes to the Church in the city of Philippi (4:5). He is not one of those "doom and gloom" preachers, whose only message seems to be a harsh-sounding announcement saying, "The end is near!" Of course, the Lord's coming in almighty judgment at the end of the world is imminent—it could arrive at any day. He will separate the sheep and the goats, welcoming the one group into the full blessings of the Father and sending the other into eternal punishment. But Paul looks at Christ's coming with rejoicing because it means that the suffering believers' final vindication is about to happen. He had already told them, writing from captivity and facing an uncertain future in the present life, that to depart and be with Christ is far better. To welcome our Savior's return would also be a blessed privilege for us in His Church if the Last Day comes while we are still alive.

As we are reminded in the season of Advent, the coming of Jesus is not merely about the last judgment in the future. The Lord is at hand also in a present-tense way. In Matthew 28, He promised to be with us always. He accomplishes that through His gifts of Baptism, the preaching of the Word, and Holy Communion. When we get it into our minds that God is not distant but rather ever-present with us, our actions, words, attitudes, and even prayers will reflect the rejoicing that Paul enjoined so strongly that he wanted to say it again!

Prayer, in fact, ties together all the other thoughts, words, and deeds of Christians in their life of sanctification. When we let our requests be made known to God, we thereby commend everything else about us and those for whom we pray into His hands. God is not ignorant about our needs, of course; for as we already have seen, prayer was given for our benefit and not for the benefit of our Father. Our thanksgiving to God through Christ is constantly accompanying our requests because through the blessing of the Gospel, we have received His peace that surpasses all understanding. If our sins had not been forgiven totally by grace and paid in the blood of Christ, then that peace would never have guarded our hearts and minds (Philippians 4:7).

So, knowing that the Lord is at hand, both in the present and in the (perhaps) near future, we present ourselves and everything with which we associate as holy and dedicated to Him. Timothy was commanded as a pastor to pray with and for the Church in his particular location as well as to embrace everything that God created as good. Prayer, which is always combined with the believer's meditation on the Word of God, is in our New Testament era the divinely commanded way to make everything holy and dedicated to the Lord.

5 From Words You Say, to a Way You Live (Joshua 1:6–9; Jude 24–25)

Admittedly, prayer is immensely important to Muslims. Their attention to their piety is well disciplined, and it is evident that the practice of prayer permeates a Muslim's entire life. Five times a day is the requirement. In a style that is reminiscent of Daniel praying in exile, they orient their bodies toward their common focus of holiness, the *mihrab*. The pictures of a white-clad mass of pilgrims circling and bowing to their holy shrine in Mecca are impressive, to say the least. Maybe they have something, even if it's just a tiny lesson in prayer piety and reverence, to teach to us Christians.

To be sure, we cannot take the claims of Islam seriously or regard their prayer as if it were no different from Christian prayer. Muhammad denied and even condemned the deity of Jesus Christ, and so also the religion of Islam fully rejects the death and resurrection of the world's one and only Savior, as they themselves would be proud to tell you. Because of this lack of true faith, Muslims lack true prayer. Even Martin Luther knew this and wrote on several occasions about the religion of "the Turks."

What they do have, and what they execute so devotedly in their public and private life, is a well-regimented rule for approaching Allah with praises and pleas. Without the Gospel and forgiveness in Christ, all that remains for them is the law, and that's even the natural law, not the perfect Law of God as revealed in Scripture. Their sincerity and even their notable contributions to the common good still get them no closer to heaven. But Muslims continue to try as they listen for their call to prayer (if they are near a mosque), turn toward Mecca, and bow down with ceremonial precision and utmost devotion.

We Christians have a precious treasure in the Gospel, and yet how often it is that we just sit on it and do nothing! Ceremony, bowing, certain observed times—none of those are required of us. We are the ones who truly have been set free from works and the condemnation of the Law. Our Father has commanded us to pray, but our prayer is drastically different from that of the non-Christian. True prayer that is offered to God the Father, Son, and Holy Spirit is not a forced requirement but a joyful privilege; at least, it should be. Why is it, then, that we give in to our sinful nature so readily and neglect prayer or refuse to do good works for our neighbor along with other fruits of faith? We do suffer more attacks from the devil than unbelievers do, simply because they are already his. The baptized Christian is the evil one's utter enemy. But our flesh is opposing us in our life of prayer and piety too.

However, all is not lost. We could, by God's grace, let the love of Christ compel us to pray with even greater fervor than those who think they must do it to appease their god. If we are willing to stop and appreciate the great wealth that is lavished on us by our Lord and Savior, then we in the one Holy Christian Church may yet taste of the full benefits of prayer. But even if we never do in this life, it is these benefits, guaranteed to us by Jesus Himself, that we'll see perfectly in heaven.

Conclusion

As you studied prayer these past few weeks, you might have found that you were, in fact, studying faith. There is more to the art of prayer than knowing how to do it, what to say, and why it is important. If your Christian life is going to extend beyond a one-hour session of "going through the motions" on Sundays, then prayer will certainly play a part.

Good, solid theology has never been a matter of mere academic exercise. Once faith becomes only "book knowledge," problems are sure to arise. And faithful, pious Christians know this because they are searching for insight wherever they may find it. But so many popular Christian spirituality self-help books ignore sound, biblical theology in preference to mere emotional, how-to topics. When they address the topic of prayer, the waters have already been muddied with legalism beyond drinkability (Ezekiel 34:18).

The more conservative reaction to this, though it may have a proper focus on Scripture and doctrine, still can tend to shy away from saying too much about prayer. Perhaps this is because we don't want to make it into a work that earns anything from God. I hope that in your recent study of His Word, you have found that you can study sound theology and have a fervent prayer life at the same time!

Concluding Activities

Conclude the session with an appropriate prayer and announce the next LifeLight topic.

Small-Group Leaders Material

Prayer's True Foundation

Selected Passages

Preparing for the Session

Central Focus

Prayer is a common spiritual topic these days. Prayer is best seen primarily as a God-given gift bestowed upon the baptized Christian, and not a mere legalistic duty by which we can get what we want out of God. Jesus' own example provides us a valuable window into what He intends for our life of prayer.

Objectives

That participants, led by the Holy Spirit working through God's Word, will

1. learn the baptismal ground and wellspring of prayer;

2. recognize prayer as a gift and privilege rooted in God's command; and

3. find the scriptural basis for confidence when they pray to the heavenly Father.

For the Small-Group Leader

Small-Group Discussion Helps

Day 1

1. Peter's sermon states that following the forgiveness that comes through the salutary washing of Holy Baptism come the blessings of the Holy Spirit, the inclusion of all people—including children—in the promise of salvation, and the gracious call of the Lord to Himself. Paul adds that Baptism releases one from the guardianship of the Law and claims the believer as God's son through faith. This is done as God covers us with Christ as a garment of pure righteousness and claims for us by faith the inheritance promised to all of Abraham's offspring.

2. Baptism effects a death to sin that frees us from sin's domination. Not only is this a death in us, but it is also Christ's own death worked in us daily. We identify fully with Him and all that He did for us, especially His resurrection, which causes us to walk in newness of life. This experience of dying and rising is what animates our prayer, providing its content and occasion.

3. Naaman objected to the Prophet Elisha's simple word, "Go and wash in the Jordan." He was too important not to be fussed over by the man of God himself. He believed that his hometown rivers were so much better than the muddy, tiny Jordan. But Naaman's servants, by pointing out how simple the directions were, convinced him of the power of God's Word attached to common water. This highlights the power of Baptism, which is simply God's Word attached to ordinary water, and it turns our attention to prayer because it is also a simple thing to which the Lord has attached a magnificent promise to hear.

4. Luke reports that at His Baptism, Jesus was praying, and then the heavens were opened, the Holy Spirit descended, and the Father pronounced His good pleasure. This helps not only to solidify the work of Jesus and prayer, a common theme in Luke, but also to inform us that Baptism and prayer go hand in hand. The heavens are opened to us and the Father is pleased with His children for the sake of Christ when, by the help of the Holy Spirit, we pray in the confidence of faith that has been bestowed upon us by the triune God in Holy Baptism.

5. As Paul speaks to husbands and wives, instructing them to love and respect each other in mutual submission, he says he is really unfolding the mystery of Christ and His baptismal acts of grace for the sake of His Church. Through Baptism, He cleanses His Bride and presents her to Himself without spot or wrinkle. In prayer, the Christian submits to His love, that is, receives the love and blessing that God has already promised to give in Christ.

Day 2

6. Already in Exodus (19:6), the people of God were called to be a "kingdom of priests and a holy nation." This distinction is to this day extended in Christ apart from good works to all who believe in Him, not (as

Paul's Judaizing antagonists insisted) to those who submit to the old covenant's ceremonies, especially circumcision.

7. Possible choices for similarities: sacrifice, pardon through the blood of sacrifice for sins, prayer for others, responsibility for faithfulness to God's covenant, set apart or "ordained" to do their task, God's mouthpiece to speak for God to others.

Possible choices for differences: animals no longer used for sacrifice; priesthood not passed along by human birth; male and female included in the New Testament priesthood; priests now offer their own lives in service to their neighbor for their spiritual sacrifice; the Savior is no longer a future, promised One but has already come; Jesus is the true, permanent, and once-for-all offering to God, and it is His blood that grants the pardon that Christians announce to one another; pastors are now called by God to proclaim God's Word and give out forgiveness publicly on behalf of every believer; prayer for others is now addressed by Christians directly to the Father through Christ without the need for any other human intermediary.

8. The phrase "born of God" is found in John's Gospel and first epistle, and it is equivalent to "born again." Those who are born of God have been rescued from the body of death and transferred to the kingdom of heaven. They are no longer enslaved to sin, and they have the needed help of the Holy Spirit to resist the desires of the flesh that continue to attack the believer. The Christian does not effect his own rebirth; it must necessarily come "from above," that is, from God's gracious action toward the believer in Baptism. This does not make Baptism out to be some sort of good work without which God cannot give eternal life (see Mark 16:16), but we must not on that account despise or omit Baptism due to the many wonderful promises that come true for the believer in it.

9. While God is aware of all things, including a non-Christian's attempt at prayer, He does not hear and respond to it in the same way He has promised to hear the Christian's prayer. The new birth that comes from hearing the Gospel of Christ and believing God's Word by the power of the Holy Spirit is that which takes place through a specific means: Baptism. Prayer has not been instituted by God as a Means of Grace, but rather as an exercise and fruit of the faith that He gives solely by grace. This removes all doubt in our Christian mind, because anything we do, including prayer, is open to condemnation by God's Law as sinful, self-centered, or weak. Prayer for faith or salvation erroneously assumes that faith already exists in the non-Christian's heart. The unbeliever indeed has an avenue to everlasting life, not through an attempt to come to God on his own terms, but through denial to self and full reliance on Jesus Christ.

10. Jesus is Himself the true mercy seat. Or, to put this assertion in another form, the ark's mercy seat and its role in the atonement for the sins of the people points as a type or prophetic sign to Christ. He offers His own lifeblood as the once-for-all atonement that appeases God's wrath toward our sins, brings us with Him before the Father's face of blessing, and makes our prayers acceptable before the throne of heaven.

Day 3

11. The unnamed disciple noticed Jesus praying in a "certain place." This indicates that our Lord regularly prayed and carefully selected even the location where He engaged in this noticeably important activity. The other reason, strikingly it would seem, is that John the Baptist also taught his own disciples to pray. While there was some overlap between the two circles of disciples, it is clear that John taught prayer as part of his ministry of preparation for the advent of Jesus.

12. John instructed the crowds who came for Baptism to share out of their abundance with those who were in need. Tax collectors were not to collect extra for their personal benefit at others' expense. Soldiers were taught not to abuse their power and despise their compensation. As these people returned to their particular callings, they may have prayed for God's help in fulfilling these duties, understanding that by virtue of their Baptism, they had already been granted salvation. We likewise in our vocations can proceed with the same confidence of our Father's favor and commend those to His merciful hand whom we are called to serve as His instruments in daily life.

13. Some of Jesus' recorded times of prayer were by Himself in a secluded place, like when He received news of John the Baptist's death. He, in His full humanity, in the state of humiliation, was turning to the Father for the strength that He needed. Other times, He prayed in the hearing of other people, like His priestly prayer of John 17, in which He speaks of His disciples and petitions for divine guidance as they set out to preach His Word, or when He spoke to the Father and He responded, even though some in attendance had heard

only a thundering sound. While emulating the example of Jesus has its limits, especially when compared to believing in Him for forgiveness and eternal life, which is the true center of Christianity, it is still helpful to learn from Jesus' example of prayer when we live a life that is shaped by Christ the crucified.

14. When Jesus sent word back to John in prison, He encouraged him by the marvelous works that even his own disciples could see: the blind see, the lame walk, lepers are cleansed, the deaf hear, dead are raised, and the poor (including all those who are "poor in spirit" [Matthew 5:3]) have good news preached to them. Christ's words after the envoys leave tell us that even the greatest prophet suffers from real attacks of disappointment when God's answers to our prayers are not what we think they should be. Though we in the kingdom of heaven occasionally suffer violence in various forms at the hands of the world, our ears must remain tuned to the words Jesus says to us.

15. John the Baptist had said all along that Jesus was coming and that He was greater, so that even the menial task of untying the Lord's sandals would be too great for him. He leaped for joy in the womb when Mary, carrying Jesus *in utero*, visited his mother Elizabeth. The bridegroom has come; the best man rejoices and steps aside. His work, including his Baptism and instruction on prayer, had come to an end, and it was Jesus' time to be heard. As late as Acts 19:1–7, we hear about John's influence, because the nascent Christians in Ephesus, due to the slightly less-than-accurate initial message of Apollos, said they had heard only of "John's baptism." They weren't heretics; they just needed the transition that, if it were possible, John would have been happy to provide to them personally: "Behold, the Lamb of God, who takes away the sin of the world!" (John 1:29). The natural inclination of man to the Law tends to resonate more with John's message of repentance, but our faith should remain focused not on our works of penitence but on Jesus, our Savior, who reveals Himself to us in the Gospel.

Day 4

16. When God commands His people to pray, He is giving them a gift, an offer of comfort. Commandments carry threats of punishment, and they are intended to kill our sinful nature. Prayer is the Lord's invitation to receive life in the name of Jesus.

17. These differences in Matthew and Luke, as well as the slightly different versions of the Lord's Prayer itself, need not cause concern. Several different ancient manuscripts have been consulted to produce the translation we have in our Bibles, plus it is possible, as *The Lutheran Study Bible* note for Luke 11:2–4 suggests, that Jesus taught the Lord's Prayer on several occasions. *Both* saying this prayer word for word *and* using it as a model for all other prayer is scriptural and part of Christ's command.

18. Answers may vary, but mention should be made about how the Christian who prays the Lord's Prayer can be confident, without doubt, that his prayer is acceptable to God, since God is always pleased with His own Word. Everything we pray to the Lord, even if we choose the words ourselves, is based in some way on a prior promise that He has made to us. Luther even encourages us to pray as we read and study God's Word, using the words He provides and reflecting them back to Him.

19. The three fruits of faith that Jesus mentions in this part of His Sermon on the Mount are giving to those in need, praying, and fasting. Each time, He says, "*When* you give/pray/fast . . . ," assuming that we will do these things as a helpful and regular practice for our everyday Christian life. These activities will yield great rewards when they are done in secret, that is, without hope of attention or earthly gain. They are meant to strengthen our own faith and reliance upon the Lord. They aren't required works to merit our salvation, but these things would be noticeably missing from the growth and preservation of our faith if we were to neglect them. Public prayer is not to be discouraged because of this passage, but the emphasis should properly be on the prayer, rather than the "public."

20. James repeats a divine command that anyone who would ask for wisdom must ask God in faith, without doubt. By ourselves, this is impossible; we can do so only by the Holy Spirit. If one refuses to believe or is resigned to believe anything he hears or feels rather than what God has said, then that is not prayer—it does not fulfill God's command because there is no faith. One who asks God in humility can trust in Him who gives generously without reproach, because it is the Lord who grants the faith that is required in the command to pray.

Day 5

21. The first illuminating example Jesus uses is of the man who goes to his friend for bread at midnight. The

disciples are asked that, if they ever didsuch a thing, what would they expect from their friend? A noble friend would honor the request, and more. After encouraging them to ask, seek, and knock, Jesus turns it around with the other story. He points out to the fathers among His hearers that certainly they would act with love and care toward their own children. God our heavenly Father, who is so much greater in His love toward us, will provide us that much more.

22. This is a difficult issue in the study of prayer. We have our limited, human, and self-centered perspectives governing our assessments of our prayers and God's answers. When Jesus encourages believers to ask, seek, and knock, He is not granting carte blanche for them to obtain from God all their personal desires and whims. Rather, He is appealing to their new nature as believers; and for them to continue in their faith and do the good works that the Lord has prepared in advance for them to do, they will need to pray for the Holy Spirit's aid. A so-called unanswered prayer is not a punishment or a result of some fault, but it is instead an experiential teaching from above that we must rely solely on the will and promise of God.

23. Psalm 91 has several promises of God's protection. He is a shelter, refuge, fortress, and deliverer. Attacks from any enemy, both small and great, will not come near the believer who entrusts himself to the Lord. While the righteous will see His salvation, the wicked will get their just "reward" or consequences, so we need not fret over how they may seem to prevail now at the moment. Satan used verses 11–12 when he tempted Jesus in the desert, but note how in verse 13 the "serpent" will be trampled underfoot! With such strong assurances of divine shelter, this psalm fits in very well with the moments before going to bed, and it may have provided some inspiration for Luther's evening prayer in his Small Catechism.

24. Because Elijah was drawing a sharp distinction between the false god Baal, which had certain promises of fertility, and the Lord, the true God of Israel, he appealed to the ancient promises that were made to the patriarchs Abraham, Isaac, and Jacob. "That this people may know," that is, be entirely convinced by experience, and "that You have turned their hearts back," namely, since God has already granted them faith, He is now with this miraculous event going to fan that faith into flame, so to speak!

25. Our Lord promises to provide all that we need, contentment for what we have, and strength to endure all suffering that He deems necessary. This is, in fact, the background to the well-known verse "I can do all things through Him who strengthens me" (Philippians 4:13). In this vein, God's provision of blessings that last into eternity is without bounds, "far more abundantly than all that we ask or think" (Ephesians 3:20). Encourage the class to share examples of what they would ask for the sake of another. At times, this can be clearer to us than even what we think we should ask for ourselves.

Prayer's Liturgical Shape

Selected Passages

Preparing for the Session

Central Focus

This lesson will explore the rich treasure that a liturgical heritage brings to prayer. From psalms to catechism to the Sunday Divine Service and the seasons of the Church Year, we have a wealth of material from which we can construct our own daily prayer routine.

Objectives

That participants, led by the Holy Spirit working through God's Word, will

1. analyze and employ the historic liturgy's collect structure;

2. utilize the Psalter for prayer's structure and content; and

3. construct a daily prayer practice that stems from the Church's worship life together.

For the Small-Group Leader

Small-Group Discussion Helps

Day 1

1. The impossible question that Solomon raises is, how can God dwell on earth when all the heavens cannot contain Him? (v. 27). The rest of Solomon's prayer resolves this by asking the Lord to hear the prayers of those who pray toward the temple, and to forgive them. John answers Solomon's conundrum by speaking of Christ, the Word, God's Son, who came to dwell on earth in the "tabernacle" of His human flesh.

2. Answers may vary. Most of the instances mentioned in Solomon's prayer involve calling upon God's name, whether in an oath (Third and Eighth Commandments), a confession of national or personal sin (Fifth Petition of the Lord's Prayer; Confession), relief from famine or plague (First Article of the Creed), or, in the case of the foreigner who hears of God's renown, to spread faith in the one true God to all nations (Third Article of the Creed). Several times in his prayer, Solomon pleads ahead of time for the Lord to hear, and also to forgive, when people pray in these various situations. The repetitive formula of Solomon's prayer may be compared to the form of the Litany (*LSB*, pp. 288–89).

3. The apostles' teaching, or doctrine, is heard today in the reading of God's Word and the pastor's sermon. Fellowship (Greek *koinonia*) means receiving the Lord's gifts together as one, especially in connection with the breaking of the bread (the Lord's Supper). The ESV follows the Greek by including the definite article "the" in the phrase "the prayers," suggesting that certain prayers were prayed in a common liturgical setting by these baptized members of the newly established Christian Church.

4. The sacrifice of praise is the fruit of lips that confess (or give thanks) to the name of Jesus, through whose self-sacrifice we are forgiven and made holy. The sacrifices of doing good deeds and sharing with others come as a result of confessing Christ's name, and only by virtue of faith is God pleased with them.

5. Answers will vary from person to person. Examples may point to the idea of the Church as family (v. 15), the promise of the Spirit's strength (v. 16), the indwelling of Christ (v. 17), or trust in the Lord's ability to do over and above what we ask or think (v. 20).

Day 2

6. The Church Year centers on the life and work of Jesus Christ (Advent to Ascension) as well as His continuing work in the Church by the Holy Spirit until He returns again (Pentecost to the Last Sunday). The readings over a year keep us conversant with all key teachings spread out through the whole Bible, but particular concentration and emphasis are properly laid on the most significant works of God. For example, Jesus' suffering and death is proclaimed all year, but is emphasized in Lent and Holy Week.

7. Answers should highlight significant Christmas

themes such as incarnation (God's promise to come in human flesh), the kingly line of David fulfilled in the birth of Christ, the lowliness of Jesus in serving humanity, the urge to tell the good news of salvation, and the joy of heaven and all angels at the birth of God's Son. Christmas hymns that could help pick out emphasized themes include "Angels We Have Heard on High," "O Come, All Ye Faithful," "Joy to the World," and "Hark! The Herald Angels Sing."

8. The story of Abraham and Isaac on Mount Moriah shines a light on Christ's substitution for our sake. That is, He would die the death we should have died, not far from the very site where a ram was substituted for Isaac centuries before. The great love of God the Father for us, so great that He offered up His only Son for us, prompts us to admit our self-centered sinful behavior and trust in the Lord, who will provide Christ as our sacrifice.

9. Just as Jesus Christ rose victorious on the third day following His suffering and death, so the white-robed faithful emerge from tribulation to dwell before the blessed throne of God forevermore. Though we pray now with tears, we shall have our eyes wiped dry when the Lamb leads us to the fountains of living water.

10. God directed Moses and Israel, in Deuteronomy 5:15, that the intended purpose of observing the Sabbath is to remember that God brought His people out of slavery in Egypt "with a mighty hand and an outstretched arm." Jesus' calling Himself "lord of the Sabbath" in Matthew 12:8 does not conflict with the command to observe the Sabbath; rather, it draws attention to His mighty works and causes us to behold His outstretched arms on the cross. These worked together for our salvation, peace, and true Sabbath rest (as discussed in Hebrews 3–4). The various observances of the Church Year strike a balance between tracing the mighty works of God in Christ and their application to the life and work of the Church.

Day 3

11. The Law of the Lord in Psalms is more than moral directions and "how tos." It is God's total instruction—including Gospel with the Law—that gives us life (119:109), uprightness of heart (1:1; 119:110–12), justification before God's judgment seat (1:5), and a reviving touch in time of trial (1:6; 119:107).

12. Jesus Christ is the Lord Himself who with His holy arm has gained victory for us (98:1, 3). His righteousness is plain for us in the Scriptures and in His death and resurrection (98:2, 9; 118:17–18, 21–24). Though He was chastened severely for our sake, He was not given over to the grasp of death (118:18). He is rather the stone the builders rejected that has become the chief cornerstone. By faith in Jesus, the faithful find the gates of righteousness open for them to enter in (118:19). Other psalms for study include 2, 67, 102, and 145.

13. Psalm 139 begins as an acknowledgment of the Lord's omnipresence. God knows, that is, He is intimately and experientially aware of, all thoughts, words, and deeds, even before we are aware of them ourselves. David expresses his confidence in knowing that his Creator has been with him wherever he was, even from the time when he was in his mother's womb. The well-known verses 13–16 especially describe for us the wonder of life before birth. But then in verse 19, the mood suddenly changes when David calls down destruction and even hatred against the Lord's enemies! The love toward God turns to anger against those who reject Him. We may share these thoughts in our personal experience of the cross in our life, and as we pray, we should unload these burdens before the Lord, praying, of course, along with the psalmist, "Search me, O God, . . . and lead me in the way everlasting!" (vv. 23–24).

14. There is more in Psalm 22 that refers to Jesus than just the first verse. In vivid language, particularly in verses 6–8 and 14–18, the scene and events of the crucifixion are described about a thousand years before they happen. Other parts of this thirty-one-verse psalm are statements of trust in the Lord, who is enthroned on the praises of Israel. While Psalm 23 remains completely a one-on-one prayer of peaceful confidence in Christ our Shepherd, Psalm 22 begins with the personal point of view in the face of persecution and suffering, then expands to include the spread of God's righteousness all over the world and to coming generations. The two psalms actually complement each other quite well. Students may have a preference for certain occasions for each psalm, but take this opportunity to recall their liturgical uses (Psalm 22 on Good Friday; Psalm 23 for Good Shepherd Sunday during the season of Easter and at funerals) to see that the wisdom of Christian tradition can also be applied to personal devotion.

15. Encourage students to share their composed prayers. As time and circumstances dictate, you can either have them speak them aloud or submit them in written form to be read anonymously. If someone is struggling with this exercise, offer some help in addressing a word or promise of God from the particular psalm; then offer

a simple prayer of thanksgiving or petition based on it. For more assistance, you may want to prepare for this session by consulting the lectures corresponding to Days 1 and 4 of this lesson and applying the format of the collect as well as Luther's counsel to Master Peter on how to pray.

Day 4

16. According to Paul in 2 Timothy 3:16–17, Scripture is useful for teaching, reproof, correction, and training in righteousness, and it equips us for every good work. Just like all of these activities, prayer demonstrates the presence of faith in our hearts. These actions by themselves did nothing to put faith in our hearts—that was done for us by God's grace alone. None of the works we do (including prayer) save us, nor are they considered good because we have done them. What saves us is the faith in Christ that we have been given, and it is in this faith that our use of God's Word (including prayer) can be considered as a good work in the eyes of the Lord.

17. As we meditate carefully on the story of the healing of the centurion's servant, we find Jesus, who had offered to come and heal the paralyzed man personally, standing amazed at the faith that He created by the Holy Spirit in the heart of this Gentile. As the centurion believed He could, Jesus said the word, and the servant was healed from afar at that same moment. He performed this same kind of miracle also for another Gentile, the Canaanite woman of Matthew 15.21–28. Christ teaches us that He has divine authority to heal by the speaking of His Word, even though, before and after this event, we witness that His touch cleanses the leprous man and bids the fever to depart from Peter's mother-in-law. We may reflect further and think of all that His Word does for us in our lives today. He informs us that great faith clings to that Word above all other divine blessings.

18. Matthew quotes the prophet Isaiah, from the song of the Suffering Servant in chapter 53, "He took our illnesses and bore our diseases." This is how Jesus is healing diseases and casting out demons and even raising the dead during His state of humiliation. He takes all of these vile by-products of sin into Himself, just as He does for me now as I read His Word and pray to Him. For this I owe Him great thanks, that although I was unworthy for Him to come to me, He has nevertheless decreed by the highest authority that I should be forgiven and rescued from death and damnation forever.

19. You may decide to ask the class simply whether or not this account of the centurion brought anything up. The students need to be assured that a confession is respected as a private matter, and that the content of this answer may be appropriately reserved for a one-on-one setting with the pastor or another Christian. This exercise is meant for the student to practice one of the "strands" of which Luther speaks in his letter on how a Christian is to pray on one's own (talked about in today's lecture).

20. Answers may vary. Here are two possibilities that utilize this four-stranded prayer model:

a. Lord Jesus Christ, You have power and authority over all things. I thank You that Your Word alone brings forgiveness and healing to me. I admit that I have abused the vocation and authority that You have granted to me, serving only my selfish desires. Please forgive and strengthen me that I may grant mercy to those who depend on me in my calling. Amen.

b. Heavenly Father, by Your Holy Spirit You grant the faith in my heart that trusts in Christ for eternal salvation. All glory belongs to You for this, Your great love for me and all believers from east to west. Lord, I confess that I am not worthy of Your favor, nor have I been constant in prayer, asking for Your blessing like I should, but I beg You to show Your mercy and say only the word, and my soul will be healed, through the merit of Jesus Christ, my Savior. Amen.

And a prayer that follows the five-part collect format could go like this:

c. O Lord God, as the centurion believed, so was his servant healed upon the very word of Jesus. Grant us, by Your almighty authority, Your eternal mercy both for us and for those for whom we pray, so that we all together may praise You in the kingdom of heaven, through the same Jesus Christ, our Lord. Amen.

Day 5

21. The plague with which the Lord afflicted Israel on account of David's sin came to a halt near the threshing floor belonging to a man named Araunah (or Ornan). God sent His prophet to announce to the king that the altar to the Lord should be erected there and, according to 1 Chronicles 21–22, Solomon's temple was later built on the same site.

22. David refuses Araunah's generous offer because, "I will not offer burnt offerings to the LORD my God that cost me nothing." Just as the Lord sacrificed His only-

begotten Son to forgive the sins of the world, so we are inspired by faith in Christ to respond to His love with a genuine offering of thanks. Likewise, our regular time of Scripture and prayer should be a high priority, because the Lord's blessings to us are also quite valuable gifts that we should treasure.

23. Daniel knelt and faced Jerusalem when he prayed three times a day because of the Lord's promise to be present at the temple, a promise going back to its dedication by King Solomon (1 Kings 8). Though he faced persecution on account of this routine, Daniel believed in the promise of a Savior, whom we know and confess to be Jesus Christ. Once Christ came and fulfilled the ancient promises of the Old Testament, He gave every baptized Christian the Holy Spirit, who dwells within our hearts and makes our bodies His temple. Gestures and other prayer "ceremonies" on our part do not modify anything or make our prayers any more acceptable to God.

24. Answers may vary. In Jude specifically, there is encouragement to stay rooted in God's Word in the face of spiritual battles against the sinful world. Regular prayer, while it may not be by itself a Means of Grace, nevertheless follows right along with meditating on Scripture, which builds us up in our most holy faith (v. 20). If we have neglected prayer for a time, in our repentant return to our Father we are still assured of the mercy of our Lord Jesus Christ that leads to eternal life (v. 21).

25. Encourage class members to share ideas with one another on what time of the day is best for different parts of their prayer routine. Some possible practices that some may choose to add include morning Bible reading and prayer, writing a journal, reading the Psalms straight through in a month or according to a schedule, including specific petitions that were mentioned in the church service the previous Sunday, reading devotionally the next Sunday's church service lessons, giving thanks before *and after* a meal, and praying with a spouse, family member or child before bedtime.

Prayer's True Power

Selected Passages

Preparing for the Session

Central Focus

We now begin to look more closely at the Lord's Prayer itself and apply each petition to all prayers that we may offer. We pray to hallow God's name because it was His name that was placed upon us Christians at our Baptism. His kingdom comes not because we ask or bring it about by our efforts, but because He has promised us His Holy Spirit, who enables us to believe, live, and pray.

Objectives

That participants, led by the Holy Spirit working through God's Word, will

1. connect God's triune name to our Father's commands and promises for prayer;

2. recall the Holy Spirit's work in creating and sustaining the faith in believers, and

3. distinguish theologies of glory and of the cross, secular and sacred kingdoms.

For the Small-Group Leader

Small-Group Discussion Helps

Day 1

1. When Paul addressed the Athenians, he preached the good news to them because although their philosophers may have respected the one true God, they called Him "the unknown god." All people from all nations on earth have God as their Father, in the sense that He created all people and He gives them life and existence every day. However, it is still true that there are many who are in the dark, helplessly wandering with their hands out to feel their way. To know God our heavenly Father in His love toward us, we need more than natural knowledge. We need what God provides by His gracious hand: Jesus Christ, the Word of salvation, the promise of resurrection and life everlasting. With these blessings, our Father becomes truly known to us.

2. The curse that God attached to eating the fruit of the forbidden tree meant that Adam and Eve would one day die. But the Lord God was also protecting them from sealing their sinful state upon their own heads forever. Now that they had knowledge (that is, experience) of evil, eternity would mean permanent separation from God. Access to the tree of life is granted to those who have washed their robes in the forgiving blood of Jesus the Lamb, according to the final vision of Revelation. (See the hymn "The Tree of Life," *LSB* 561).

3. Peter's simple prayer to Jesus was "Lord, save me!" It was borne out of his immediate need for rescue from the wind and waves overpowering him. As little as his faith was, Peter at least recognized his utter helplessness and turned to Christ alone. After pulling the disciple out from certain drowning, Jesus placed him back in the boat and got in Himself. The Church has long been compared to a boat, blessed with the presence of Christ on board as we gather to worship Him and receive His gifts.

4. The Old Testament saints had faith in Christ also, thanks to the promise of Satan's defeat by a Savior, the seed of the woman, in Genesis 3:15. Without this first promise, there would have been no faith, no prayer, no coming to the Father for anyone.

5. Isaiah laments over Israel's poor condition. It is as though God never established or ruled over them (63:19). He must have hardened their hearts (like Pharaoh) to punish them with their own stubborn, sinful, and faithless attitudes (63:17), and, grieved in His Holy Spirit, became their enemy instead of Savior. They need God to remember His promises and act because He is good and acts with love and pity. Ancestors such as Abraham and Israel are long dead—they cannot be petitioned for help—the Lord alone is their only hope of salvation (63:16). Isaiah appeals to God's mighty

name: he calls God the potter for us, the clay (64:8); he pleads for Him to have regard for the beautiful temple that now lies in fire and ruin (64:11); and he points out that when the Lord rends the heavens open wide, all the earth, even the mighty mountains, tremble at His presence (64:1).

sense of privilege that our Lord has given us to call upon this same name with thanksgiving and petitions. Prayer is a truly holy task, and we are privileged to engage in it. Realizing this for ourselves helps us pray in our weaknesses and in times of discouragement. We have an inside line to the universe's ruler!

Day 2

6. Moses was concerned that the Israelites would not believe him. He thought he needed something more to lend credibility to God's message of salvation. Ever gracious, even to those of weak faith, the Lord revealed His holy name: "I AM WHO I AM." As Jesus would remind us later in Matthew 22:31–32, "I am the God of Abraham, and the God of Isaac, and the God of Jacob" is backed by all the promises and acts of mercy that were witnessed by those patriarchs.

7. The other miracles at the burning bush further impress God's name upon Moses to remove his doubt and fear that he expressed upon the hearing of his assignment. The snake prompted him to flee, and a diseased hand would have given immediate cause for concern, yet with a simple word, God restored both to their original state. Reading these accounts may put the thought in our minds to ask God for signs when we face a decision or difficult trial, but we have no less of the power of God's name than Moses received on Mount Sinai, plus the already fulfilled death and resurrection of Christ, now revealed to us in Scripture.

8. "I am" comes straight from Exodus 3:14, when God revealed His holy name to Moses, and Jesus was claiming this holy name for Himself, unmistakably calling Himself God. His miracles, and finally His resurrection, would demonstrate this to be true for all times and places, just as He did for Moses at the burning bush.

9. As Jesus came down to earth from His heavenly throne, He temporarily laid aside His rightful glory and "did not count equality with God a thing to be grasped" (v. 6), that is, something He could use for selfish gain. In His state of humiliation, He not only became man, but He also took on the form of a servant so that for our sake He could suffer even death on a cross. Having completed this holy mission given Him from the Father, Christ ended His time of humiliation by being exalted and receiving, now as God *and man,* the name above every name.

10. When we recall Paul's words about the exalted name of Jesus, at which every knee will bow, we renew our

Day 3

11. In John 14, Jesus promises the Helper, the most prominent title that He uses for the Holy Spirit. The word in Greek is *parakletos,* which is sometimes put into English as "Paraclete" (pronounced PAIR-a-cleat). When taken all together, these other translations of this word get at its full sense: Exhorter, Comforter, Mediator, Counselor, and Advocate. He uses the pronoun "He" to make sure there's no mistake about the Holy Spirit's unity in the Godhead with the Father and the Son. And He is the Spirit of truth, to indicate the content of what He will impart to the Church—pure truth straight from the Father and the Son.

12. Our mind and emotions process everything that comes to us from the world. Jesus is clear that His peace, which the Holy Spirit imparts, is not of the world. Emotions are God-given blessings, and we can have good feelings from time to time about our Father's love toward us, but they never are to be our sole indicator of that love. Everything in us, including our thoughts and emotions, are tainted with self-focus and sin. Like everything else about us, our feelings need to be guided by the pure truth of God's Word. The Holy Spirit, according to Jesus, teaches us all the things that Jesus wants us to learn about Him and gives us an accurate picture of the love He gives us from the Father.

13. The Holy Spirit's work is described in John 16 as convicting the world concerning sin, righteousness, and judgment. While the world (Greek *kosmos*) is defined in John's writings as mankind in its state of unbelief, it is also the object of God's love (John 3:16). These convictions of the Law are intended to bring unbelief, even the unbelief inside our own souls, out of darkness into the light of day. Once we are convicted of our own sin of unbelief and reliance upon the world, which will one day pass away in judgment, we can, by the Spirit's power, turn to Christ for His righteousness, which alone saves us. Thus, in this way, He enriches our faith and prayer life.

14. Prayer is mentioned in Joel's Pentecost prophecy when he says, "Everyone who calls on the name of the

Lord shall be saved" (Joel 2:32; quoted in Acts 2:21). Prayer is not a cause of faith, like a meritorious work, but a sign that the Holy Spirit has granted faith in the hearts of those who pray, because they are calling on God's name. All the miraculous signs that were seen at Pentecost in Jerusalem were not for their own sake; rather they pointed to the existence of faith in all believers, male and female.

15. Christ promised that the Holy Spirit's help will be available to His disciples whenever they are called upon to testify to the truth before rulers and authorities. At those trying times, believers will have their anxious hearts comforted by the Spirit. Confessing the truth is a fruit of faith that will be spoken at certain times to other people. Prayer is likewise a fruit of faith, where we confess the truth regularly and give our praise and requests directly to God. So the Holy Spirit's occasional help in one goes hand in hand with His constant assistance in the other.

Day 4

16. As God in His almighty glory passes by Moses, proclaiming His name, "The Lord," He must cover Moses with His hand while Moses stands in the rocky cleft. This keeps Moses from seeing God's face; when that hand is taken away, the man of God is allowed to see His back. God's reason is "man shall not see Me and live." So to come near to man, God must hide Himself and allow only His back to be seen.

17. The Aaronic Benediction is an extraordinary gift of grace. The unapproachable glory of God's face is made to shine on faithful believers because the Lord is pleased to put His name on them. This, too, is a hidden glory, just as it was for Moses in the rock. Through Christ, the image of the invisible God (Colossians 1:15), this blessing comes to us today when it is pronounced by the pastor at the end of the Divine Service.

18. Pop spirituality, if it ever gets around to mentioning Christ, does so only so that people get a good feeling about themselves or personal fulfillment for their life here and now. Better relationships and temporal success tend to crowd out the spiritual blessings of forgiveness, resurrection, and eternal life. When Paul says that we are "most to be pitied" if we hope in Christ "in this life only," he is convicting the modern-day popular lust for self-centered purpose, not the cross-focused faith.

19. When a Christian goes through a difficult trial, no matter how strong or mature that person's faith is, the feeling often comes to mind, "Why is God doing this to me?" It is very difficult to "count it all joy," as James counsels, because suffering is not joyful in our human experience. While your words of comfort may take on different forms, depending on whether the trial is physical, emotional, a result of being sinned against, or a matter of guilt over a previous sin, you could point the person to the grace of Jesus Christ, who has fully endured all suffering for us and grants us steadfastness and peace. It would also be a good idea to invite this person to church and, if the person is a communicant, the blessing of the Lord's Supper.

20. Even though Job never sinned when he seemed to throw up his hands in the face of his extraordinary affliction, he still approached his situation as though God were capricious in His activity toward man. Job's loathing of his own life is understandable, but a bit uncomfortable in our ears (3:3, 11; 10:1–3). His friends were intent on pushing the angle that Job was suffering for sins he had committed, especially in 15:5; 22:4; and 35:1–6. But Job learns more than God's sovereignty and power; he finds out that God is his Redeemer (19:25) who reveals true wisdom to man (28:28) and who forgives by grace upon Job's prayer for his errant friends, just as He did for Job's children at the beginning. So by the end of the book (42:1–6), along with the greater temporal blessings, Job discovered the fuller perspective of God's activity known as the theology of the cross.

Day 5

21. While Pontius Pilate infers that there are many accusations, all unfounded, that the Jewish crowds testify against Jesus, the main charge, it seems, centers around His claim to be "the King of the Jews." This was the longest-running controversy of Christ's earthly life, going all the way back to when the Wise Men visited Herod, wishing to see the one "born king of the Jews" (Matthew 2:2). John 19:10 reports a bit more of Pilate's examination of this claim, not to get a guilty plea so much as to find a way for Jesus to go free. When his loyalty to Caesar was questioned because of his just actions, however, Pilate was forced to relent. In Matthew, we read that he symbolically washed his hands of the wrongdoing that he saw he could no longer restrain.

22. The governing authorities, according to Paul in Romans 13, are instituted and established by God. Jesus Himself recognizes Pilate's God-given authority, but reminds him that such great power is not a matter to be taken lightly. It is such a weighty responsibility that

Pilate's pronouncement of innocence can be taken as the Father's own acceptance of Christ's sacrifice, about to be completed on the cross, as that of a truly innocent victim. That, along with the fact that Pontius Pilate and the crucifixion that he ordered is attested to in world history, is the reason why his name appears in Christianity's creeds.

23. Psalm 82:1–5 is addressed to those who in this world administer justice as God's instruments, so in occupying this vocation, whether they are believers or not, they are called "gods" and "sons of the Most High." Verses 6–7 seem to be a pronouncement from God Himself, and verse 8 concludes the psalm with a petition to the Lord. Their limits are their very lives (v. 7): because of God's place of prominence among the assembly of His "divine council" (v. 1), and because they have neglected their divine duties, they are limited by Christ's own appointed time of judgment over the whole earth and His direct inheritance of all nations.

24. Peter and the other apostles were repeatedly told by legitimate temple authorities (who "sit on Moses' seat," as Jesus pointed out in Matthew 23:2) not to teach in the name of Jesus, prompting their reply that God's authority overrules theirs. If there is an immediate instance of a contradiction between man's law and God's, there can be no question in the Christian's mind at that moment of whose law must stand. But we must also be aware of those matters that tend to whittle away ever so slightly at God's Law and, by small degrees over stretches of time, overthrow it eventually. If it is merely a question of injustice toward us, then we make our appeal to proper earthly authority, as Paul did when he appealed to Caesar based on his Roman citizenship. At all times, we are to keep in mind that the spiritual kingdom remains superior to the secular, even though normally their spheres and duties do not fully overlap.

25. As we honor those who have been set over us in the Lord, we are also called to commend them to God in prayer. We pray for their health, safety, and wisdom, but in bringing them before the throne of grace, we also hand them over to His judgment, to which all earthly authority is subject. In prayer, we remember the coming of the Last Day, when the almighty king will set all rulers aside and execute all rights pertaining to Himself as the ultimate ruler! Prayer also strengthens us in those times of trial and reviling, because we call upon the same Savior who suffered all injustice yet entrusted Himself to the Father, that we might die to sin and live to righteousness.

Prayer's Outcome: Thy Will Be Done

Selected Passages

Preparing for the Session

Central Focus

Our limited, human, and sin-plagued perspective can make it difficult to assess, and even accept, God's will. This lesson will not only shed light on what exactly it means to seek our Father's will, but it will also lead students to discover in Scripture how the Holy Spirit conforms our will to His.

Objectives

That participants, led by the Holy Spirit working through God's Word, will

1. discern properly what God's will is over against the will of the three spiritual enemies;

2. revisit the example of Jesus, specifically in His praying, "Thy will be done"; and

3. rejoice in the Spirit's work of keeping them steadfast in Word and faith.

For the Small-Group Leader

Small-Group Discussion Helps

Day 1

1. These narratives tell about Gideon and the fleece, Saul finding out that Jonathan disobeyed, Saul consulting the medium, and Matthias being chosen. Most of the time, lots were the means of determining a yes-or-no answer. Those who were earnestly seeking God's will, such as Gideon and the eleven apostles, began their decision-making procedure with a prayer for God's choice to be revealed. Even though Saul had made a rash vow to kill anyone who ate a lick before he said so, he still followed the priest's advice and prayed for the Lord's guidance. When Saul consulted the medium, he clearly rejected God and was rebuked not by a mere spirit but by the dead Samuel himself in an exceptional circumstance that has no equal anywhere else in Scripture.

2. The biblical accounts of lot-casting, using the Urim and Thummim, even of the soldiers throwing dice at the cross to get Jesus' garment, are all related to the progress of salvation history up to the death and resurrection of Christ. The apostles rightly saw their selection of a twelfth as divinely necessary to fulfill the Scripture that they had quoted concerning Judas. Once Christ ascended and the Holy Spirit was given out to the New Testament Church, the Lord's mission of salvation took on a new phase. Just as the old ceremonies are fulfilled and no longer necessary, so also are we free in the Gospel as we seek God's will. Casting lots is still honored among some Christians, but divine sovereignty should not be overemphasized to the detriment of justification by grace. Whatever method of choice is considered, prayer to the Lord for His will should always accompany our efforts.

3. Nathan the prophet had no direct word from the Lord, so when David proposed to build a temple to replace the tabernacle, he said, "Go, do all that is in your heart, for the LORD is with you." Jesus is called Immanuel, meaning "God with us," to emphasize His constant, forgiving presence among His redeemed people. Because of Him, we have a renewed heart, complete with pure desires to accomplish God's will and serve others. Nathan had to revise his counsel to David upon receiving a direct revelation from the Lord, but this was more because God desired to announce that His promised Messiah would come from the house, that is, the lineage, of David.

4. The Holy Spirit intercedes for us; that is, He approaches the Father on our behalf, speaking for us in "groanings too deep for words." We do not know what to pray for, due to our weakness, namely, our struggle of the renewed nature against our sinful flesh. Although we cannot escape our Lord's scrutiny, which searches our hearts, we can be confident that the Holy Spirit will pray perfectly for God's will for us, as He does for all the saints.

5. The statement "all things work together for good" is

sometimes difficult to take, especially if one is presently going through a time of suffering. Words of comfort to another Christian would be sure to emphasize God's constant presence, Christ's identifying with us in every way, and His promise that our sufferings now are not worth comparing to our future glory (see v. 18). These comforts in Romans 8 are intended only for the Christian, since Paul is here describing God's gracious activity to those whom He has called to faith in Christ. When Jesus says that God makes the sun shine on good and evil alike, He is speaking instead about God's general providence to all people, without any specific reference to final salvation.

Day 2

6. In preparation for the account of the flood, Moses writes that God saw that every intention of man's heart was only evil all the time. Sin has corrupted the image of God in the heart of man, so that his will is now set against the Lord's will. When Seth's birth is recounted, the phrase "in God's image" now changes to "[Adam] fathered a son in his own likeness, after his image." This passing on of human traits and personal characteristics from parents to children also includes the transmission of original sin, as well as a corrupt will, from which we can be set free only through Jesus Christ.

7. Paul describes a struggle that Christians face within themselves: we do the very thing we hate to do. We know that God's Law condemns sin, and we have the desire to do what is good and in accord with God's will, but we have no power within us to carry it out. In our flesh, the sinful nature, we are enslaved to sin. In what Paul calls our "inner being" or "new man," we agree with God's will and rejoice in it, knowing that Christ has delivered us from this body of death. Our hope of rescue from this struggle is realized when at death our soul is finally separated from the flesh and goes to be with the Lord. In this intermediate state, about which only a little is written directly in Scripture, we the faithful await the resurrection at the Last Day, when body will rejoin with soul for life everlasting.

8. Before and after each of the earlier plagues, Moses gave Pharaoh an opportunity to comply with God's will that the Israelites should be let go from Egypt. At first, the record is clear to say that Pharaoh refused the request and hardened his own heart. At chapter 10 and following, we begin to see that, in light of Pharaoh's consistent and stubborn refusals, the Lord hardened his heart, which is to say that for him, there would be no further opportunity for repentance. He will now have to abide permanently by a decision that remains his responsibility. God is going to bring glory to His magnificent saving act by bringing this confirmed enemy to justice.

9. When Abraham speaks to the Lord concerning His planned overthrow of Sodom, he is humble, appealing to God's justice rather than his own rights, and pleading for the Lord to set aside any anger that Abraham would deserve for his boldness. Abraham looks to be bargaining with God, narrowing down his request by fives and then tens of people. We should not take this as a mandate to offer God any works of our own in exchange for His favor, both because of the biblical principle of grace alone and because we need not doubt that His will is always done for our good. Note all the hardship that still visited Lot in his escape, even though at the same time God was rescuing him from utter destruction.

10. God compares His will to ours as "higher than the heavens are above the earth." But He assures us that His will is always centered in His mercy and compassion toward us, constantly eager to receive us back from the ways of our errant, human will. We are confident in this because He has revealed it in His Word, which will not return to Him void. When blessings come to us that are easily discerned and in agreement with what we want, then we might find it easy to give God the glory for His love, as we certainly ought. But when hardship comes, or when blessings are harder to spot, then these words from Isaiah call us to repentance and lead us back to what our Father tells us is most important.

Day 3

11. When Jesus prays in the Garden of Gethsemane on the Mount of Olives, He requests that the cup be removed from Him. Drinking this cup meant enduring the suffering and death of the cross. The previous mention of a cup was in the first Lord's Supper in the upper room: "This cup that is poured out for you is the new covenant in My blood" (v. 20).

12. Jeremiah's discourse about the cup of the Lord's wrath helps us understand more clearly Christ's prayer in Gethsemane. Not only was Jesus to go through intense physical suffering and crucifixion, but He was also destined to drink this cup of divine wrath toward sin, a wrath that is powerful enough to destroy many nations. In 1 Corinthians, Paul speaks about the cup of blessing, which is the cup of the Lord's Supper, the

blood of Christ shed for the forgiveness of sins. Because Jesus drank the cup of God's wrath, He poured out His lifeblood for our eternal blessing. But the Lord's wrath is not annulled, and if one refuses to believe, thereby drinking this cup in an unworthy manner, then, Paul says, that person drinks judgment, a synonym for wrath, on himself.

13. We should not take Jesus' words "not as I will" to mean that He had previously desired something different from what the Father wanted. On the contrary, these words are recorded in the Gospels to emphasize that He was perfectly in line with the Father's will. He is under the Father and subordinate to Him not because the Son is less than the Father, but rather because He is still in the state of humiliation, or the form of a servant (Philippians 2:7). He temporarily set aside His rights as the eternal Son of God so that the divine plan of salvation would come to fruition in His suffering, death, and resurrection.

14. Though our Lord's words to His disciples in between His times of prayer sound like scolding, He is actually strengthening them for the upcoming time of trial. He encourages them to watch and pray because the task of praying Christians is to keep watch against the attacks of sin. Even if we should fall from that task, our merciful Savior promises never to forsake us, just as He did for His disciples mere moments before His Passion began.

15. Although the exact words "Thy will be done" are not mentioned in Jesus' high priestly prayer, the theme of those words is reflected in these specific petition phrases: "glorify Your Son that the Son may glorify You"; "I . . . accomplished the work that You gave Me to do"; "I have manifested Your name"; "I have given them the words that You gave Me"; "You sent Me"; "I am coming to You"; "I have guarded them"; "that the Scripture might be fulfilled"; "[not to] take them out of the world, but . . . keep them from the evil one"; "sanctify them"; "I have sent them into the world"; "that they may be one"; "that the love with which You have loved Me may be in them, and I in them."

Day 4

16. Satan's will is crafty and, as Jesus warns, this ancient foe has been the father of lies from the very beginning. He resents it when God's people would enjoy even the smallest blessing, to the extent that he roams and paces lionlike through the world seeking to devour his next victim. He lays a snare to catch the less-than-vigilant, so that they may be duped into performing his evil will.

17. The best defense against both the sinful attraction to and persecution from the world is to shed the light of God's truth over against its darkness. Ecclesiastes derides the shimmer that the world has to offer as mere vanity, and the toil that the world loves is meaningless unless it can be considered a gift from the heavenly Father. Ishmael persecuted Isaac, but it was the promise of God in Scripture that casts out that which would try to enslave us to the ways of the sinful world—a sinful world that, John reminds us, is passing away. The world can infiltrate the church too—so much so that Jesus predicted the hour (whether in the time of the apostles or in our time) when those who kill His followers will think that they are doing God-pleasing work. But the help of the Holy Spirit is Christ's own gift that will keep us from falling away on account of the world.

18. Galatians 5:17–21 is very clear about what exactly are the works that give us evidence of the influence of the sinful nature. The next few verses are just as clear when Paul speaks of the fruit of the Spirit. When sinful works turn us from setting our minds on things of God to the things that are hostile to Him, then a dirty, impure feeling may arise because of the crushing condemnation of the Law. That's what David admitted in Psalm 51, when he pleaded to the Lord for cleansing and for a pure heart. Since Christ knows what is in man, He is eager to hear our prayers and comfort us with the Gospel truth that there is now no condemnation.

19. Paul cites all three spiritual enemies in connection with the Ephesians' former condition of being dead in trespasses and sins, beginning with the world. The course that the world runs in its state of degeneration is a course of death. The world follows the devil because he is master over the sons of disobedience, meaning they have been imprinted in their very nature with the inevitable bondage of sin that is passed from one generation to the other. These children of wrath have controlling desires of body and mind that drive their everyday lives to carry those desires out.

20. The devil is described as "the prince of the power of the air," denoting his spiritual power and control over us on earth. Christ is "seated . . . in the heavenly places," which means He has obtained all power and authority following His ascension to the right hand of the Father. Whereas formerly under the devil we were locked in subservient bondage, in Christ we are seated with Him following our resurrection, ruling with God's immeasurable riches at our fingertips. He made us alive when

formerly we were dead. All of this is summed up in the phrase in verse 8: "by grace you have been saved."

Day 5

21. First, God provided physical strength to Elijah as he was fleeing the death-threat of Jezebel. Leaving his servant behind in the city of Beersheba, Elijah proceeded alone in the desert. With the restful shade of a broom tree and super-strengthening food from the hand of the angel of the Lord, the prophet made it to the mountain where it all had started for Moses—not to forget that it took him forty days and forty nights to get there. Then, not too far from where that burning bush had been, Elijah saw the wind, earthquake, and fire. Once he heard the whisper, he received comfort in his upcoming assignments. He was even granted his own replacement in Elisha (notice how the other two men, whom Elijah will anoint, have swords, but Elisha will "put to death" by a greater means, namely, the power of the Word of God). The greatest long-term comfort is the objective fact laid out for Elijah that a remnant of seven thousand true believers has been set aside all along, in response to his complaint of being the only one left.

22. God's will, as described to the Thessalonians, is the believers' sanctification, that is, their being made holy every day, free from their former bondage to lusts and anger. The positive commands in 5:16–22 are descriptions of how God is doing His work in the hearts of His faithful. This is evident in the blessing (vv. 23–24), in which it is made clear that the God of peace "Himself" will bring about this complete sanctification. Finally, when Paul requests their prayers in verse 25, he is both acknowledging his need for God's help along with them and giving them their holy, priestly work of prayer, which unites and strengthens all Christians according to the Lord's will.

23. Jesus says He came not to do His own will, but that of the Father. It's not that the Son's will would be any different from the Father's; rather, Christ is emphasizing that He is in perfect unity with the Father and is committed to do His will. God the Holy Trinity alone ensures that all of the elect will believe in Jesus and be raised on the Last Day.

24. The phrases "washing of regeneration and renewal" and "born again to a living hope" are clear New Testament references to Baptism. These passages expressly state that this sacrament is solely the work of God in the one who is baptized. In granting the gift and constant comfort of Baptism, the Lord accomplishes His will to strengthen Christians and keep them firm in the faith, confirming to them that they are heirs of a permanent, heavenly salvation.

25. Revelation's vision of the great white-robed multitude carrying palm branches depicts the perfect and final fulfillment of God's will. Verses 1–7 tell us that the number of those sealed and preserved to eternal life is 144,000. This is not literal, but it stands for every believer from every time and every place. Not one of our Lord's precious children is missing from this scene, so this passage is a picture of you and your loved ones in the faith, along with all believers from every tribe and nation. No matter what tribulation they may have suffered in earthly life, the saints have washed their robes in Christ's blood from every stain of sin, and all of the world's curses of sin, from hunger to heat to every last tear that is shed, will be completely and permanently removed. You may wish to mention this Bible passage's prominence at the festival of All Saints' Day and that *Lutheran Service Book* (p. xxiii) suggests it to be read on the occasion of a national or local tragedy.

Prayer's Nourishment for the Traveler

Selected Passages

Preparing for the Session

Central Focus

Daily bread is everywhere! As Luther pointed out, praying for it doesn't actually make it come to us, but rather our prayer leads us to realize that God provides us everything we need for this body and life. When we pay attention to the unique part that we play in the several roles of our Christian vocation, our hearts may be filled with genuine thanksgiving to our ever-provident God.

Objectives

That participants, led by the Holy Spirit working through God's Word, will

1. review all to which the phrase "daily bread" refers in our lives and how God provides it;

2. address any concerns about "selfishly" asking the Lord for daily bread; and

3. receive personal encouragement from what Scripture describes as Christian vocation.

For the Small-Group Leader

Small-Group Discussion Helps

Day 1

1. Anxiety is a sign of "little faith," but not yet a lost cause. When Jesus says, "Do not be anxious," He is giving a precious gift: in His very speaking these words, He is overcoming the anxiety that is plaguing His hearer. Eating, drinking, and clothing are needs that easily cause us concern. But when He points to two of the most fleeting things in all of creation, namely birds and grass, He assures us of our daily bread with the rhetorical question, "Will He not much more" take care of you?

2. The greater blessing is the kingdom of God, faith in Christ that grows stronger when we rely on Him all the more and look to ourselves less. "And all these things" in verse 33 refers to lesser gifts that we receive from our heavenly Father. Even though He knows we still need this daily bread for the present life, He grants them in addition to our most important need, that is, our spiritual need of eternal salvation.

3. Even though God already knows and has answered our prayers before we pray, He has still commanded us to pray. He loves His own promises coming back to His ears from the lips of His faithful. Prayer helps us, in anything for which we pray, to believe that we have already received it. This way, it never becomes a pious wish or a guess; anything that our heavenly Father wants for us, we will have when and where it pleases Him.

4. Although verse 16 has a close connection with the immediately preceding verses on temptation, it rightly points out that we should not be deceived when it comes to discerning the true source of every good and perfect gift. God is called the "Father of lights," meaning light itself has its origin in Him, so there is no darkness or change in Him. His ultimate purpose in blessing us with daily bread is rooted in His will to bring us forth in faith as His firstfruits of harvest.

5. Paul's words in Romans 8 are an excellent encouragement to those who think their prayers have turned cold, or who have stopped praying altogether. The Holy Spirit prays continually for us, expressing perfectly in inexpressible groans the very things that we have trouble getting out of our inmost hearts, since we can use only human words.

Day 2

6. The wicked shall not prosper forever; the words about this in Psalm 1 help us interpret the lamenting psalms, such as 94, which complain to God about the apparent prosperity of the faithless. The cry of "How long?" gives us a clue to the hope of future judgment and vindication for the Lord's people. Current problems are thrown in the Father's face along with a plea for Him to remember and fulfill His good and lasting promises. Praying these psalms will go a long way in helping us deal with situations where it seems that evil is going to win.

7. Peter was reminding his flock that they are in the last days, just as we are now. Our Lord's delay, which is insignificant considering that with Him a thousand years are as though they were a day, is expressly for the elect's sake. He wishes that all should reach repentance, and so He allows the scoffers (who cast doubt on the coming of the Lord's justice) to stand for a while longer. The example of Noah and the flood has been used by Peter before (e.g., 1 Peter 3), and it serves his purpose in comforting his readers in their current frustration with the ungodly "getting away with it."

8. From the hand of God comes the believer's true enjoyment in the eating and drinking of daily life, and confidence that these are true blessings from His hand. Those without faith, called "sinner" here in this portion of Ecclesiastes, gather and collect temporal blessings, but these will get passed on down to someone else eventually. There's no greater thing for them (i.e., salvation), so they're left frustrated with the nagging idea, "Is this all there is?" In Ecclesiastes 3:1–8, the poem on "times" demonstrates how everything on earth has its season and must come to an end, but the Lord and His promises last forever.

9. David fears God's Word over everything because, fallen though he is from grace, Saul is still the Lord's anointed (Hebrew: *mashiach*, or *messiah*), and his demise must come from the Lord's hand. David cuts a corner off Saul's royal robes to prove his claim and seal his word that he has had no intention of killing Saul. David is a man after God's own heart (1 Samuel 13:14), and so his actions reveal how the Lord is ever patient, even with those who have rejected Him. When the Amalekite declares that he obeyed Saul's order to kill him, David executed him, again because of his utter respect for God's Word concerning His anointed.

10. God's mercy to all people certainly owes to His almighty power and His general qualities of love and mercy. But we would be missing the point of it all if we were to exclude from this equation His saving mission in Jesus Christ for all people. He is the God who *in Christ* justifies the wicked. He had mercy to Paul, "chief of sinners" though he was, specifically so that in Paul the apostle, *our Savior* could display His perfect patience. And it isn't enough to say that God is such a "nice guy" that He holds out a pious wish for everyone to be saved. Rather, it must be pointed out at the same time that there is one and only one mediator to do the job: the man *Christ Jesus*, who gave Himself as a ransom for all.

Day 3

11. The two trees in Genesis had no significance in and of themselves, except that they were part of God's good creation, they were placed in the middle of the Garden, and their fruit was good for food and pleasing to look at. Even the tree of the knowledge of good and evil was not a bad or poisonous tree, because sin did not have its origin in the fruit itself. These trees are God's means because He attached His Word and promise to their fruit. By eating, or refraining from eating, man would bear fruit of his love and devotion to God, his Creator, because these actions were governed by His Word. The serpent knew the power of God's Word attached to means, and so he twisted the curse and made it seem desirable, luring Adam and Eve to consider their own desires above God's Word, thereby falling into sin.

12. The use of means requires faith, and serving as a case in point is the story of Moses striking the rock with the staff when the Lord said only to speak to it while holding the staff. The Lord pointed out the mistake was not in Moses tripping up on a tiny detail, nor is it a moral lesson about acting rashly out of frustration, but rather the necessity is in aligning one's actions with God's Word so that He alone receives glory whenever He gives a blessing through means. God chooses His own means in order to bless us; we dare not make Him conform to our notions.

13. Lest anyone be mistaken and think Naaman's leprosy was healed by the Jordan's water alone, this account of Gehazi would set the record straight. Naaman had been healed by God's Word, which was attached to the water. When Gehazi lied out of greed and disobeyed God's Word given through Elisha, even though Naaman was eager to give some form of gratitude, that same Word of God attached Naaman's leprosy onto Gehazi and his children, this time without the use of any other means besides Elisha's own words.

14. Our merciful Father uses plain and lowly means (including other people) to give great blessing and daily bread to us, and likewise Jesus informs us in His depiction of the Last Judgment that even our lowliest service to the most insignificant-looking of people is counted by grace as rendering high service to Him. Sheep and goats alike in this story are amazed at how they acted (or refused to act) on opportunities that they did not even realize were there. The "least of these" serves as a means to serve Christ Himself.

15. Answers may vary. These psalms provide several ex-

amples in nature (similar to when Jesus speaks about sparrows and lilies of the field) about how God provides for the needs of otherwise helpless animals and plants. He gives to everyone, man included, their food and drink in due season. As an example, it may look to some like it is raining, but the psalmist understands that it is God's own gracious visitation (65:9). His mighty voice both strips bare and gives life. He provides strength and protection to whole nations, and others who depend on their own might are left desolate. In praying for daily bread, we look for God's many means of providing it, and Luther helps us out in his Catechism answer to the question, *What is meant by daily bread?*

Day 4

16. Ephesians 2 is very clear that our salvation is by grace, not by works. Grace is not a "thing" that God gives us so that we will then do the things that will make Him accept us into heaven. It is instead His undeserved favor, earned fully for us by Christ in His life, death, and resurrection. Good works are fruits of that grace; they're what we have been created to do. Once we have been renewed in the image of Jesus, the Son of God, we proceed with the works that God had prepared in advance (or called us) to do. This is our individual vocation as Christians, not to earn eternal life, but because we already have it.

17. Government and authority are established by God. Even the most godless ruler is in place only by God's say so. Electing our leaders is a special blessing by which our Lord uses us as His tools to do His will in the left-hand kingdom. Our duty to all authorities is to submit to their rule, call them to account if anything they do forces one to act in a manner displeasing to God, judge their actions according to sound reason, and reprove, if necessary, with love and respect. Most of all, we owe it to our leaders to pray for them. Our government has no further obligation toward Christians than to do its God-given duty for all people. The government's duty is to punish the wicked and commend those who do good things. While God may use the government as an instrument, He is still the one who paves the way for the Church to save sinners, so all glory belongs to Him alone.

18. Aside from the slavery question, where it is only mentioned in passing that such an arrangement is incompatible with the Gospel, Paul wrote this letter to let the grace of God move the heart of Philemon to accept back his former slave. Christian love and the work of the Christian in his or her vocation can never be forced by law or requirements. Whereas before, we were enslaved in sin and had to be goaded and prodded by threat of punishment to do what was right, now that we are set free by the forgiveness of sins, we are gently compelled by our own love for others to serve our neighbor in whatever calling our Father has given us.

19. The greatest talents and the most earth-shattering faith all come to nothing if there is no Christian love. Everything comes to the believer through the love of Christ, and so everything done in the context of someone's particular vocation proceeds from the new nature that is filled with that same love. This does not stop merely at gratitude for what the Lord has done for us, but it certainly includes that. The love that is described in this famous passage is something that is impossible for us, but with God, all things are possible.

20. Answers will vary. *Example:* O Lord my God, You have called me to my particular role in my family, and I thank you for the people that You have put into my life. I admit that I have sometimes taken them for granted, and I have even hurt them, which is just as much an offense against You. Forgive me for the sake of Christ, and fill me with love, understanding, patience, and kind words for these Your people, and bless whatever I do to be a blessing to them. In Jesus' name I pray. Amen.

Day 5

21. Christ Himself gave strength to the apostle Paul through all times. It took some long, hard lessons, but he learned contentment through what he suffered so that he could face any situation with the confidence that God would supply his every need. A Christian can gain this same confidence through the Word, a thoughtful moment with a fellow believer, and the forgiveness of sins that is handed out in the preaching of the Word (public and private) as well as in the Lord's Supper.

22. As Paul rebukes the Corinthians for paying higher regard to human strengths and prestige, he boasts in the things that people normally would despise. With his theology of the cross going full blast, the apostle is downright proud of every misfortune, unfair punishment, and painful heartbreak because he knows he belongs to the Lord and that he is engaged in His holy work.

23. When times are difficult, the circumstances may be quite an ordeal to bear, but the lesson of being content

in the Lord is usually made quite plain to us. When our situation is easier on us, the truths of Scripture need to be sought out diligently, so that we remind ourselves with Job that we can't take it with us. Times of suffering are useful tools that God can use to bring us closer to Him, but whether we're dealing with good or bad experiences, we must never forget to pray and meditate on His Word.

24. In Psalm 118, there is an abundance of both thanksgiving and petition for help. Students may be encouraged to share what is particularly helpful to them. Note how the antiphon in verses 1 and 29 serves as a frame for the entire psalm. That can be both a thanksgiving and a prompt to turn all burdens and cares to the Lord, "for His steadfast love endures forever!" Test Him on this! Take refuge in Him who is your salvation!

25. Thankfulness is mentioned three separate times, scattered throughout this section in Colossians as an essential ingredient to all Christians' fulfillment of their daily calling, both individually and especially together as the Body of Christ. With thankful hearts, believers bear with one another, forgive, sing, pray and do everything else in the name of Jesus. It is through Him and in His once-for-all sacrifice for us that we offer our thanks up to the Father.

Prayer's Reliance on Forgiveness

Selected Passages

Preparing for the Session

Central Focus

Forgiveness of sins is granted in Baptism, but it is also applied whenever the Christian hears the Word of Christ in the Gospel and receives forgiveness and strengthening of faith in the Lord's Supper. Thus forgiven, Christians confidently pray to their heavenly Father and are ready to forgive and pray for their neighbor.

Objectives

That participants, led by the Holy Spirit working through God's Word, will

1. make the connection between forgiveness, prayer, and the Christian life;

2. utilize the biblical principles of Law and Gospel in personal prayer; and

3. apply the power of forgiveness to their prayers for their needs and as they pray for others.

For the Small-Group Leader

Small-Group Discussion Helps

Day 1

1. The Epistle to the Romans discusses the necessary faith for salvation and faith's distinctive expression, in 10:13: "Everyone who calls on the name of the Lord will be saved." Taken alone, this statement sounds like a condition or demand is being placed on us. It seems as though we must pray or we must confess Jesus Christ before we can have faith, but it's actually the other way around. In the context of the rest of this passage, the ability to call upon the Lord in prayer clearly comes as a gift through hearing the Gospel, especially verse 17, "faith comes from hearing," the preaching of forgiveness in Christ.

2. Pastors have a call from God to proclaim God's Word and hand out His gifts in the forgiveness of sins and the Sacraments. The Lord bestows this call using the Church, usually the Christian congregation. With God's call comes His Gospel promise of courage and constant presence, even in the face of evil attacks, provided the pastor remains faithful to preach only the Lord's Word. Similarly, when all Christians pray and live their life under grace, the Law can have no condemnation. We have the confidence to approach the Lord because of His gracious promise to us all in Baptism.

3. The teachings of Law and Gospel in Scripture need to be divided and distinguished because they are opposites in relation to each other. If one is used in order to do the other's task, then the Word is corrupted and the salvation that God means to impart through the Bible is overturned. When prayer is built on a confusion of Law and Gospel, then it does not express true faith properly. Sound words taken from Scripture itself do not make prayer into a collection of magical syllables, but they convey the correct understanding so that prayer is fully benefiting from our Father's Gospel promises.

4. The Law points out every attempt to use works or sacrifice as ridiculous. Micah uses hyperbole to prove a point: though one could perhaps sacrifice a thousand rams and pour out tens of thousands of rivers of oil, or even—at the utter extreme—sacrifice the very children one has borne, it wouldn't be enough to approach God as though one were on equal terms with Him. Rather, by grace alone, our Lord informs us of the works of the Law with which He is pleased, not our attempts to pay our own way. The sacrifices of the Old Testament were never instituted for their own sake, but to awaken faith in the coming Messiah, Jesus. *Example prayer:* O Lord, You have shown me what is good in Your sight, yet I refrain and try things my way instead. Forgive me through the precious blood of Jesus, and bring me into Your kingdom according to Your promise.

5. Jonah was angry and prayed to God out of frustration when he realized that God was not going to destroy the evil city of Nineveh after all. He actually resented the Lord's gracious compassion! The incident with the vine taught Jonah a lesson that revealed itself from the lesser to the greater: if Jonah could care about a single

shade vine that is here today and gone tomorrow, how much more would our Father have compassion over a whole city of people and animals that He desires to be saved? As Peter points out, God may at times look slow to us, but really He's being patient, genuinely desiring everyone's repentance. Why do some not end up repenting? We will never know the answer to that question. We do know that it takes Law *and* Gospel to create faith, and the final emphasis should be always on the Father's proper work and attitude, as depicted in the Gospel.

Day 2

6. King David prays for forgiveness concerning his "transgressions," first because he knows that one sin has led to others, including his murder of Bathsheba's husband, Uriah. Then he acknowledges that all his sins are ultimately against the Lord Himself. His sin is not merely a collection of evil deeds but a sinful condition in which he lived even in his nine months of life before birth. Praying this psalm impresses on the believer that one is in need of cleansing and the soul must be purified and renewed because of what sin has done to a person's heart.

7. In Psalm 51, the believer is confident of forgiveness because it is entirely the responsibility of God. He gives the gift of cleansing because He is a God of mercy and He acts with steadfast love (see Psalm 23:6, "goodness and mercy") that is freely provided, not earned. He purges, He washes; though He has broken bones in the crushing condemnation of the Law, He causes rejoicing because He has blotted out all iniquities. The prayer to create a clean heart, which occurs in the Divine Service liturgy at an important transitional moment between the sermon and the response of thanksgiving and prayer, is also an appeal for God to do what He has already desired to do in the penitent believer.

8. In one of the most emotionally vivid scenes in the Old Testament, Joseph reveals his identity and forgives his brothers for selling him into slavery in Egypt. He could forgive them not merely because a long time had passed and "time heals all wounds," but because Joseph was able to see God's hand behind it all for everyone's good. Though his brothers didn't know it at the time, Joseph was able to overhear their admission that they were guilty of sinning against him. Upon Judah's offer to substitute himself to become a slave in place of Benjamin (foreshadowing Judah's greater descendent, Jesus), Joseph pronounced forgiveness for all of the brothers who had sinned against him.

9. Even with Joseph's gracious words of full reconciliation with his brothers, they were afraid of retaliation from him seventeen years later when their father died. Perhaps they figured, according to selfish human wisdom, that Joseph had forgiven them only to please their father while he was still alive. Sin and the feeling of guilt can raise its ugly head even after absolution, and it is as David prayed, "My sin is ever before me" (Psalm 51:3). While it seems as though they fabricated Jacob's deathbed request to Joseph, the point really is that the brothers knew they had no worthiness in themselves to deserve forgiveness but had to resort to the plea of another on their behalf. Joseph's "Am I in the place of God?" certainly implies he is not, yet our Lord does grant His authority for mere men to hand out His forgiveness to others.

10. To approach the Lord's holy presence, one must have "clean hands and a pure heart." These requirements cannot be met by anyone, because we are born into sin and we have soiled our lives with evil deeds. But Jesus invites sinners to come to Him for prayerful rest, since He has fulfilled all requirements. Bathed in His cleansing blood and wrapped in the robe of His righteousness, we are granted access to our heavenly Father's holy face, and it is for us a face of blessing now and forever. We exchange our unbearable burden of guilt for Christ's easy burden of love.

Day 3

11. The authority given to the Church to forgive sins comes from Jesus Christ, who paid for that forgiveness. He breathes the Holy Spirit to enable all Christians to pronounce forgiveness to those who have sinned against them, no matter what their vocation. The only difference in the pastor's case is that God has called him (using the Church as His means) to the vocation of proclaiming forgiveness as his dedicated task, both in public (as in the Absolution) and in one-on-one situations. Pastors should still train and encourage Christians to forgive and gladly do good to those who sin against them in their daily lives. No matter who says it, it will always be Christ's forgiveness.

12. At both Jesus' Baptism and transfiguration, God the Father said, "This is My beloved Son, with whom I am well pleased." This pronouncement is extended through the ministry of our Lord's Church to everyone baptized into Christ. The apostles, including Peter and those with

him on the mountain, were the first to hear the Father's own words, and they were the first to occupy that office of ministry. The Father's words, "Listen to Him," also obligate preachers to teach only what Christ has given them through the Holy Spirit, not their own interpretation.

13. Nathan immediately pronounced forgiveness upon hearing David say, "I have sinned against the Lord." No further contrition or satisfaction was needed to save David's life, even though David himself admitted that he had deserved to die. Yet Nathan explained the reason why David's son must die as an earthly consequence of this sin, because the effects of sin are not always taken away by absolution.

14. Jesus is our advocate, John writes, in order to plead for our forgiveness with His own life whenever we mistakenly follow our sinful human nature. *Propitiation* means "the sacrifice offered to satisfy God's wrath against sin." Admitting our sin is saying our agreement (*confess* means "say together") with God; if we deny our sin, we call Him a liar. How then can we pray to the Lord when we have just denounced His truthfulness? His anger would otherwise still remain on us. So, honest confession and faith in His forgiveness are both essential to the Christian's prayer.

15. Answers will vary. Some great comforting points that can be found in Psalm 32 are that the Lord Himself covers sin completely; He doesn't count iniquity, though we are aware that it exists within us; He provides a time to find Him in prayer, a hiding place from trouble; He surrounds us with steadfast love. Keeping silent and neglecting to pray to God for forgiveness causes sorrow, makes one stubborn like the horse or mule, and creates the feeling of bones wasting away; but God lays the hand of His Law heavy on us so that we will confess and be released from the unnecessary burden of our sins. Absolution is offered to provide this release especially to burdened Christians, precisely so they may rejoice and be glad in the Lord, who reckons us all righteous for the sake of Jesus.

Day 4

16. The younger, prodigal son despised his father and demanded his inheritance in advance of his father's death. He wasted his generous portion of the estate, and it was unlikely that the father would get it back. The father had lost his son because he took up residence in a far country. Because of his behavior toward his father, the prodigal son ascertained rightly that he was no longer worthy to be called his son. The father, however, responded in a way similar to the characters in the other parables, in that he went to unexpected great lengths to welcome his son back. The shepherd left ninety-nine sheep to find just one, and the woman turned her house upside down to find just one coin out of ten. The father saw his younger son from a long way off and ran (risking public disgrace), showed him great affection, honored him with a robe and ring, and celebrated his return with a feast.

17. The older brother in the parable was angered first at the celebration (the fattened calf provides the best feast possible) and then at how easily his younger brother was forgiven and welcomed back. Ironically, the older brother claimed to have been a slave to his father, even though he was really the owner of everything, and it was his brother who actually became a slave in the far country. The older son disowned his brother and disrespected his father with cross words, but after Jesus gives the father's final appeal, He cuts the story short. What will the older brother do? That's up to the hearers, both the Pharisees and us, to see if forgiveness and reconciliation will prevail for all concerned.

18. The first servant owed an impossibly large debt to the king, which was forgiven out of pity. He demanded a comparatively miniscule sum from his fellow servant; when he didn't receive payment, he choked him and threw him into prison. The different amounts help us see how sins against us measure up against our sins against God. It is a helpful reminder that when we come to those times when we feel exceedingly wronged and become overtaken with the desire to lash out, then such feelings need to be kept in check.

19. The final lesson from Jesus' story in Matthew 18 is negative: if you refuse to forgive, so shall the heavenly Father do to you in judgment. It does not mean that this behavior is "more sinful" than other actions, but rather that it betrays a denial of forgiveness and even a denial of the Christian faith itself. Salvation is impossible without God-given faith, rooted in Christ-earned forgiveness. When we pray for our enemies, we know they are turned over to God. If He gives them forgiveness, then that is what should come from us also. If they still do not show us evidence of repentance, then through our prayer they still are in God's hands, but we have freed ourselves from the temptation to condemn our enemies in His place.

20. James ends his epistle with an appeal to pray.

Whether it is in suffering, out of cheerfulness, for the sake of the sick, or to forgive a fellow believer who has sinned, prayer is powerful because it proceeds from the righteousness of faith, that is, from Jesus Christ the Righteous One. Mutual confession and consolation in the Gospel is what will save a sinner who wanders from the truth. This gift of God to the Church is so powerful that it will cover a multitude of sins.

Day 5

21. When Jacob last heard from his twin brother, he had reason to believe that his life would be in danger if he ever set foot in Esau's presence. The night before, Jacob wrestled with God (the inspiration for his name, Israel) in order to strengthen him with a confirmation of the very blessing that he stole from Esau. With irony worthy of the theology of the cross, along with that spiritual strength, Jacob's hip was put out of joint, as if to put us in mind of what the Lord said to the apostle Paul, "My grace is sufficient for you, for My power is made perfect in weakness" (2 Corinthians 12:9).

22. Jacob demonstrated utter humility toward his brother, partly because he feared for his life and loved ones, but also to seek favor from Esau as though he were approaching the face of God. When he wrestled the night, he saw God's very face, and yet his life was spared. Coming before Esau, whom he had deceived years before, gave Jacob a similar experience. He had already divided into two camps, and so he presented all that was precious to him (in ascending order, it would seem, Leah followed by Rachel), he bowed seven times to show complete subjugation, and he firmly insisted that his gift not be refused.

23. In Matthew 5, the Sermon on the Mount, Jesus places an obligation on the person who remembers that someone else has something against him; for example, if I have hurt someone, I need to attempt to initiate the process of reconciliation between us. In Matthew 18, the roles are reversed and the one offended must go to his brother and show him his fault, one on one. The first example comes up in connection with an act of faith and worship, but the other direction seems to apply more to any situation in general. Answers may vary among participants as to which of the two is more difficult, along with the particular support for that choice.

24. James addresses Christians' relationships with one another in several places. The implanted Word saves the soul, giving rise to righteousness and repressing anger, making the believer quick to hear and slow to speak. Our judgment of one another ought to follow the law of liberty, which produces mercy, the Christian's dominant quality over judgment, in the same way the Gospel predominates over the Law. The tongue is controlled from cursing and trained to bless instead, making peace that overflows with a harvest of righteousness. Anger and quarreling are therefore sin when considered within the bounds of the Church, because faith knows by means of the Lord's mercy what the right thing to do is. Rather than risk our own judgment, we approach brothers and sisters in Christ with patience.

25. Ephesians 4 details to what extent the Christian puts on the new self, especially as one relates to fellow believers. Reconciliation is here commanded through the exhortations to be truthful to one's neighbor, to resolve anger issues in the same day they happen, to forgive one another as we have been forgiven through Christ, and to remove all bitterness and wrath. Anger is treated here as a given; we cannot completely avoid it. But we can manage our anger so that we do not fall into sin, that is, unbelief. The opportunity that the devil seizes upon is when the Christian has a right to be angry with someone but then, in response, harbors malice and gives in to corrupt desires over against that offending neighbor. When a family gathers together at table or toward the end of the day, they can debrief with one another concerning what is troubling each member, as well as comfort one another with forgiveness.

Prayer's Battle against Our Enemies

Selected Passages

Preparing for the Session

Central Focus

The Christian's battle, in all of life as well as in prayer, is one of defense against real spiritual enemies. But we are not left defenseless. This lesson will lead participants to find God's protection from temptation and His gift of endurance during a time of trial.

Objectives

That participants, led by the Holy Spirit working through God's Word, will

1. revisit Old Testament narratives that describe the believer's battle against temptation;

2. locate God's deliverance in Baptism and the Lord's Supper; and

3. place Christ crucified at the center of their life and prayer.

For the Small-Group Leader

Small-Group Discussion Helps

Day 1

1. Our real enemies are powerful and normally hidden from view, and to fight these spiritual forces of evil, we need the strength of the Lord's might. These are rulers, authorities, worldwide powers, forces of evil in "heavenly places," namely, in a spiritual realm normally not visible to earthly eyes. When we pray for our enemies, we are comforted that our true battle isn't against these "flesh and blood" people who may be making life difficult for us. There are bigger enemies, and our Father will work His perfect justice for us in His time.

2. The armor of God is given to the believer to be primarily defensive against the attacks of the spiritual forces of evil. Standing firm, withstanding, extinguishing flaming arrows, being ready—these are all actions of holding ground, rather than attacking. Prayer goes hand-in-hand with taking the sword of the Spirit, but it is God alone who through His Word fights for the praying Christian. Paul also asks for the Ephesians to pray for him because he is fully aware of his own role in God's battle plan, and his boldness in speaking the Word is essential.

3. Revelation portrays the devil (Satan, the accuser) in the image of a dragon, reminiscent of his serpent's form that deceived Adam, Eve, and the whole world. He attacks the believers because he was defeated by Michael and his angels in heaven and was therefore cast down to the earth along with his angels, the evil spirits. He is full of wrath following his decisive defeat, and his time before his utter, final destruction at Judgment Day is short.

4. Whether God indeed granted an exception and sent the soul of Samuel to En-dor in defiance of the witch's trickery, or whether He permitted an evil spirit simply to look like Samuel and speak to Saul an accurate prediction of his judgment and death, this incident still warns us that the spiritual realm is not a plaything. Saul had disobeyed his own previous, godly commandment, and the consequences were devastating to him and his family. Such matters may be popular in our day, but they are just as dangerous.

5. A boy is convulsed by an evil (or "unclean") spirit and Jesus heals him, but He also goes to great lengths to emphasize the necessity of faith to prevail in the battle against unseen enemies. The man said to Jesus, "If You can . . ." and upon the Lord's rebuke realized his own lack: "I believe; help my unbelief!" This says that the man has faith, but he has let his fear come up and choke it, like the weeds do with the seed that is sown, according to Jesus' parable of Mark 4. Prayer exercises faith, and it is given true power over unclean spirits, not because the believer has any innate power, but because the believer trusts solely in the power of God.

Day 2

6. Abraham had believed the Lord's first promise to

him, that he would settle in the land that God promised him and he would have descendents as many as the stars in heaven. But now that he was in his mid-80s, and his wife offered the option of her servant Hagar as a surrogate mother, Abraham conceded in a decision that revealed his doubt of God's ability to keep His promise. This produced tension in the house between the slave and free woman, as Paul describes allegorically in Galatians. Only one will receive the inheritance of the promised Savior, and that will be Sarah, along with her son, Isaac, who finally arrived thirteen years later.

7. Joseph looks like he's doing everything right. He's refusing the advances of Potiphar's wife, he's keeping himself from providing an easy pathway for this temptation, yet he is still ambushed with a situation that leads to imprisonment. This was certainly not a blessing at the time, but the Lord had the events lined up so that Joseph could ascend to his later position as governor of Egypt and become reunited with his father and brothers. Even though wemay do everything possible to avoid difficult times, when they come we can find comfort in Joseph's later words: what was intended for evil, God has used for good (see Genesis 50:20).

8. Aaron gave in to the wicked desires of the people and made the golden calf for them to worship. But to make it seem right, he attempted to call for a festival to the Lord (v. 5), which was the farthest thing from the minds of the faithless people. The holy worship of God and the base desires of the flesh are incompatible. When he was caught, Aaron tried to avoid responsibility by claiming that he had no control over the will of the people. He even credited the calf with the ability to come out of the fire by itself!

9. How ironic it is that a man of Samson's physical strength could be made weary to the point of death by Delilah's pestering! His love for her must have produced this one weakness in him that she decided to exploit. Believers who are attacked repeatedly sense that there will be no escape from the barrage unless they give in. We should pray for a heightened awareness of this temptation tactic, no matter who may try to employ it or how much it wears us down.

10. David's initial temptations led to sins that had heavier consequences, making them harder to cover up. At any point along the slippery slope, the only way out is honest confession of sin and trust in the Lord's forgiveness. King David assumed that he could maintain control of what his sins were doing, but his plans were failing miserably. He did finally come to the point where he repented, and he was restored by God's grace, but not before extensive damage, including especially the death of Uriah, had occurred.

Day 3

11. Paul connects Baptism with the idea of "putting on" Christ. This has already been explored in connection with our standing before God: in Jesus, we are counted righteous and acceptable to our Father through faith. This applies also to times when we face temptation, because our Savior faced all of them in our place, and He came away from them each time without sin. When in remembering our Baptism we continually put on the righteousness of Christ, His resistance of temptation also becomes counted in our favor.

12. Baptism seals God's promise that we are spiritually reborn "not of perishable seed but of imperishable." That is, when we suffer temptation or trial, we can be confident that when all is said and done, we will not be destroyed by the attacks of our spiritual enemies. Thanks to Baptism, which is water and the Word, we are not like withering grass or a falling flower; we have the living and abiding power of the Lord's preached Word in us.

13. Even though many followers deserted Jesus upon hearing His words, Peter claimed that for him and the Twelve, there was nobody else to whom they could go. The words of Jesus gave eternal life and faith in Him, so the very words that repelled some are the same words that, by the Father granting it through the Holy Spirit, made it impossible for others to leave.

14. John 6 ("I am the bread of life . . . whoever feeds on My flesh and drinks My blood has eternal life") may not be speaking directly and specifically about the Lord's Supper; nevertheless, the Lutheran Confessions (e.g., FC SD VII 61), while making sure to distinguish the "two types of eating," still include the believer's participation in the Sacrament under the wider topic of spiritual eating, which our Lord is describing here. By our faith, which feeds on the flesh of Christ and is strengthened in the Lord's Supper, we receive His specific promise to raise our bodies up on the Last Day. The Sacrament offers a kind of strength to our bodies that may not be felt, but it is there all the same.

15. Answers will vary. *Example:* Merciful Father, in Baptism You have rescued me from the kingdom of this world and claimed me for Your blessed kingdom now and forever. Help me to live each day as a child of light

rather than darkness, but when I stumble, restore me with Your forgiveness and assure me that the Spirit of truth will not depart from me. This I ask not because I deserve it, but according to Your promise that was made to me at the baptismal font, for the sake of all that Jesus has done for me. Amen.

Day 4

16. In Hebrews, the apostolic author cites a previous time in this congregation's early experience when suffering was especially intense. Some effects of this hard struggle have evidently lasted up to the time when the epistle was written. There was public affliction and humiliation, unjust imprisonment, seizure of property, and so on. Some people were discouraged, and so this congregation needed some help from God's Word to ensure that they would not shrink back from faith in the Lord.

17. Hebrews offers help to the Christians going through a time of suffering by speaking of it in the context of divine discipline. The author had just recited a litany of many heroes of faith in chapter 11, and now calls for them to think of these Old Testament individuals together as a "cloud of witnesses." They should also recall Christ Himself, and all of the suffering that He endured, that they should expect suffering also and not be fainthearted when it does come their way. With all that they had gone through, it puts their experience in perspective when it is mentioned that they had not yet resisted to the point of shedding blood, like other Christians in other places had. This training in the faith may have been painful at times, but these believers are promised that it will yield "the peaceful fruit of righteousness" in due time.

18. Peter assures struggling Christians in two ways: first, the enemies who persecute the righteous will not ultimately get away with it, and second, God will preserve His faithful to the end. Noah and Lot are Old Testament examples of lonely believers who were righteous in the eyes of God, even while being surrounded by a horde of violent and wicked people. Before the latter were utterly destroyed through flood, fire, and brimstone, the precious few of their families were rescued. It may not ever look like a grand, earthly victory for the Church, but God's people will still endure to the heavenly goal.

19. The Lord ordered Gideon to reduce the size of his army before they fought the powerful Midianites. In a humorous-looking spectacle, the 300 brave soldiers who lapped water like a dog became the ones chosen out of the original 22,000. This was done to prove to everyone, both the Israelites and their enemies, that God fights and wins the battles for His people. We recall His encouragement to Elijah, who thought that he was the lone believer, perhaps surprising him with the fact that the remnant of the faithful amounted to seven thousand. Yet the number is not to be considered by itself, but rather that the Lord has provided faith when and where it pleases Him.

20. In Psalm 38, David speaks about his sin in connection with his time of suffering. While we should not necessarily take from this that we, too, are suffering direct punishment for our deeds, we can still be reminded at such occasions that we ought to repent because we deserve far worse consequences for what we have done. Our sinful past may linger over us and haunt our conscience, so the best remedy is to confess and receive the salvation that the Lord desires for us. Examples may vary, but you may wish to emphasize verses such as 9, 15, 21, and 22 because they recall God's promise to hear and deliver His people.

Day 5

21. People who act out of unbelief and doubt toward the Lord are putting Christ and His love for sinners to the test, whether they lived in the times of the Old Testament, the New Testament, or today. God allows temptation to come to us in a time of testing and refining our faith; however, He attaches two important promises: first, the assurance that the temptation will not overwhelm us beyond our ability (whether we are aware of that ability or not), and second, the promise that He provides the way of escape from the temptation.

22. The burden that we bring to the Lord Jesus is not only our sin but also our crosses and struggles. He exchanges our yoke, which feels heavy and overwhelming to us, for His light burden. What the Father has hidden from the wise (who rely on knowledge and experience) and revealed to little children (who serve as examples of simple trust) is His promise to save us, despite what our experience tells us. Jesus offers release not only from sin but also from temptation and trial through Him.

23. As Abraham was about to sacrifice Isaac as an offering to the Lord, in obedience to His clear command, the Lord Himself offered the way out. Isaac had "figuratively" been killed, as Hebrews says, because Abraham's faith was firm. He believed the first promise of God

concerning Isaac so strongly that he was convinced that Isaac's death could not get in the way of the Lord's gracious will. The way of escape offered through the ram turns our attention to Christ and His sacrifice that delivers us from certain death and consoles us during difficult times.

24. Even though God is not explicitly mentioned anywhere in the canonical book of Esther, His work behind the scenes is evident, especially in the incident with Haman and his plot to exterminate the Jews. Esther's cousin Mordecai saw in her ascent to the king's inner circle an opportunity for God's rescue to come about, but only if she did not shrink back in fear. As she puts her very life at risk, her only hope for success would be the favor of the pagan king, symbolized by his extending the golden scepter, granting admission to his presence. The rest of Scripture helps us interpret the events of this unique book in light of Christ, who extends our Father's favor to us through the sacrifice of His life for us.

25. The invitation to come to the Lord, seeking Him while He may be found, is not given just to the unbelievers who need to be "saved." Christians, too, get caught with the temptation to squander their faith on something that is really not the true spiritual bread of salvation in Jesus. The missionary concern for the lost, important as it is, must never lose sight of the continual spiritual needs of the Lord's flock whom He has called to be the Church. Hurting, struggling sheep come to the Good Shepherd to benefit from the covenant of grace that He assures to all who hunger and thirst for righteousness. It is available without money and without price because Jesus paid the full price for us.

Prayer's Final Goal

Selected Passages

Preparing for the Session

Central Focus

Evil (and the evil one, Satan) desires us as its captive. Our journey through this world's valley of sorrow will, in God's own time, come to its blessed end, and our prayers today, in the midst of all of the short-term matters on our minds, should still reflect that big-picture perspective. Special emphasis will be given to the Bible's references to the believer's conscience.

Objectives

That participants, led by the Holy Spirit working through God's Word, will

1. trace the description of the conscience, especially in the New Testament epistles;

2. discover how the heavenly Father bestows a clear conscience on His children; and

3. look to the Lord's deliverance from evil in this world, and forward to the blessed end.

For the Small-Group Leader

Small-Group Discussion Helps

Day 1

1. A pure heart is not a requirement for perfection. That would involve the Law, which can do nothing for our spiritual life except point out the fact that we are sinners. It instead calls for a life that is shaped by the Gospel. God creates and gives the pure heart within the Christian. A good conscience is commonly understood only as some "inner voice" that tells you what is right and wrong, but that leaves out an important aspect: do I thoroughly believe that I am a forgiven sinner, acceptable in the sight of God? A sincere faith is not mere knowledge of Jesus but the conviction that He died and rose *for me.*

2. Aside from planting and strengthening new churches in several faraway lands, Paul's great life "project" as an apostle was to collect the offering of aid from these Gentile congregations and present the much-needed material blessings to the poor Jewish Christians in Jerusalem who had been suffering due to famine. He was striving not in a physical battle, but a spiritual one, fought on the battleground of conscience. The evil one was opposed both to Paul's Word from God and to his works of mercy, so the apostle was going to fight Satan's constant attacks. It is in this struggle that Paul requested help from the Roman Christians to pray on his behalf, and so they will fight alongside him, great distance notwithstanding. Completing his God-given task would bring Paul joy, not in his own success but in the working of the Lord through him.

3. Jesus addressed conscience in Mark 7 from the angle of clean and unclean foods. People were concerned, just as Peter was in Acts 11, about how to keep the laws of ceremonial purity. These rituals at one time governed how a person could stand before God's almighty presence. The evangelist wanted to make it clear that Christ has now, in fulfillment of the Law, declared all foods clean and that conscience is rather defiled not by neglecting a ceremony but by living out a denial of faith that occurs naturally within the sinful heart. Peter was taught through the vision he had that now God makes no distinction, as He had formerly with laws addressing ritual purity and circumcision. At the Apostolic Council in Acts 15, it was decided that the Gospel would spread to the Gentiles without these strict legal stipulations. The only concession made was to prevent any possible offense by requesting the Gentiles, out of Christian consideration, to refrain from a few of their practices.

4. The phrase "Become all things to all people," in 1 Corinthians 9:22, is often taken out of context to mean that we can let people do anything they want, as long as we're trying to save them. But Paul was adapting to those who had not yet heard anything of the Gospel and were still following their pagan ways. He would win them over when their weakness of faith was "phased

out" in deference to the true freedom of the Christian. If someone were to assert freedom in such a way as to give the appearance of condoning outright sin, then Paul would have none of it, for fear of giving opportunity for the weak brother to stumble. He allows a certain kind of diversity in matters that are neither commanded nor forbidden, but all is in honor of the Lord, that is, in full accord with God's Word. The phrase that should be taken to heart is "Whatever does not proceed from faith is sin" (Romans 14:23).

5. When Paul circumcised Timothy, it was still early in the growth of the Christian Church. And so, to remove any cause for offense or stumbling with former Jews, his young assistant was circumcised in light of the fact that it was well known that Timothy's father was a Greek. Circumcision in this case was not a denial of faith in Christ but a choice meant to bear with this group's weakness until Paul could eventually work through patient teaching to correct their false understanding. Several years later, when false teachers in Jerusalem (not weak or newly converted Christians this time) stubbornly insisted on Jewish requirements, including circumcision, for the Christians there, Paul kept them from forcing Titus to be circumcised. His reason there was to resist their efforts to replace the Gospel with slavery to false doctrine. Paul is consistent when you consider that, with both men, he was concerned about keeping the Gospel intact as well as letting it spread to as many as possible.

Day 2

6. Hebrews devotes a significantly long section, chapters 9 and 10, to the sacrifices that were commanded in the Old Testament. Very clearly, the author states, "Without the shedding of blood there is no forgiveness of sins." Along with this forgiveness of sins, there is the important concept of purity of conscience. While the temple sacrifices sanctified the believer with the blood of bulls and goats, Jesus accomplishes an even greater cleansing through His own blood. This is the reality behind the washing of rebirth and renewal that happens to the Christian through Baptism.

7. Whenever Jesus is teaching and doing miracles in the temple, the animal sacrifices serve as a fitting background for His claim to be the one and only sacrifice for the sins of the world. Even from His boyhood, He was aware of the temple as "My Father's house." The political enemies of Jesus question His authority there, especially after He cleanses the temple, and they are dumbfounded when the Lord brings up the validity of John's Baptism, which is bound up in Jesus' identity as the Son of God come in human flesh and blood to be given into death for our sins.

8. Baptism is a saving gift of God and is meant to impress upon the believer that he is fully accepted and justified in the eyes of his heavenly Father. Christ rose from the dead and took His place at heaven's almighty throne to give the blessings of forgiveness and good conscience. In Matthew 28 He promised all these benefits through Baptism in His command to His Church to baptize. Remembering your Baptism reminds you of God's assurance that Jesus is your Savior, now and forever.

9. With the warning "We must all appear before the judgment seat of Christ," Paul entreats all hearers to know for themselves what that judgment will be. This is the full idea of the Christian's conscience that works together with an accurate perception of right and wrong. Note how the apostle does not have the believer place his hope in his own conscience, because that is still imperfect and riddled with sin, just like all other fruits of faith are. Instead he says, "What we are is known to God, and I hope it is known also to your conscience." He desires for his entire flock to have in themselves the comfort of being certain of God's acceptance, but above all, he points them to the new creation that is a sure thing for them in Christ. Our Savior completed the task by reconciling the world to Himself; now His message of reconciliation spreads to the rest of the world, which needs to hear it.

10. In the Galatian circumcision controversy, the freedom of the Gospel was at risk of being lost. The false teachers were introducing this requirement as one little "extra" detail added to forgiveness, but Paul denounced this as a little "leaven" that can spread to the whole lump, that is, that will affect everything else and destroy spiritual freedom. If they were to succeed in their efforts, then a yoke of slavery would burden the believers' consciences—they would think that circumcision and the Law would be necessary for them to be convinced of their salvation. But Christ has set us free. That is our advantage that will keep us running the race well.

Day 3

11. We own our possessions, but how easy it is for our attitude toward things to enable them to own us! It is not the money that is the problem, as Paul says to Timothy, but the love of money that is the root of all kinds of

evil. It's the inordinate value we place on stuff, not the stuff itself that could lead us astray. The rich fool ended up talking to himself without paying any attention to the God who gave abundantly. But when another gift, the gift of life itself, is at stake, then the man's love of wealth was pointed out for the foolishness that it was.

12. Jesus' test of the rich young man to sell all he had was specifically to point out his sin of presuming to have perfectly kept the Law before God. For the rest of us, the counsel is to act toward wealth *as though* we had rid ourselves of all of it. We should not feel guilty of having possessions, as long as we don't stop considering them as God's gifts, in second place to the precious treasure of salvation. Riches in this life are uncertain, Paul reminds Timothy, so he should remind those "rich in this present age" to keep their hopes properly set on God and to be ready to share with those who are coheirs with them of eternal glory but are currently burdened with physical lack.

13. In this parable, one would think that Jesus has flipped on His position toward being honest! But the point of the teaching lies in how our use of God's material gifts indicates the value we place on the eternal blessings. Our time on this earth will come to an end, and the last judgment will reveal how we used the Lord's gift of faith in the fruits of good works. Just as the steward received benefit from a generosity that didn't belong to him, so also we are blessed to receive God's reward in Christ when we had no contribution to make to Him.

14. Eagerness for the best places, the need for VIP treatment, and competition for favors seems to influence us all at some point, but it is especially strong and enduring in some people. Satan can and does use this inner urge to his advantage, because people are usually willing to do just about anything for attention or fame. It is not natural to opt for the lowliest place in order to be promoted to the higher. However, that is exactly how our Savior, Jesus, achieved His power and glory, by humbling Himself to be our lowly servant.

15. In addition to the rich promises of the future resurrection of the body, God even now has in mind both to protect and rescue us physically as He grants us to pray in the Lord's Prayer. Our whole self, described in 1 Thessalonians 5:23 as "spirit and soul and body," is kept blameless by His grace until the coming of Christ. Our body is currently, and not just in the future, a temple of the Holy Spirit, sanctified and set apart through Baptism for the Lord to do His will through us. Good health is just as much a gift of the Lord, right alongside a healthy faith for the soul.

Day 4

16. Encourage students to share answers. Offer gentle helping questions such as these: What was it that made you fearful the most? What did God provide to help you through such a difficult time? Not everyone may be comfortable providing their own examples, but they might possibly share something that could have been more difficult for them to endure had it not been for the Lord's presence that gave them strength.

17. Psalm 77 is a psalm of lament, in which the psalmist brings a complaint before the Lord and calls upon His gracious promise of rescue. This is not the despair of one who has rejected God, but he does have some notable and serious questions, such as these: Will the Lord spurn forever? Has God forgotten to be gracious? Instead of letting these stomach-churning feelings build up, he lays them out before the merciful Father. He recalls that when he cries out to God, He most certainly will hear his prayer. After this initial complaint, the psalm continues in faith recounting God's past saving deeds and that the troubled believer will rest in the hope of deliverance in the end.

18. The comfort, exhortation, help, mediation, and encouragement that God the Holy Spirit gives us when we suffer affliction is the very same that we offer to fellow Christians in their time of need. Comfort is only the beginning of this loving service that we receive and provide, but it should be understood as including all the rest with it. The Holy Spirit brings Christ's sufferings to us: first the benefit of forgiveness and God's perfect righteousness that He earned for us, and then with it the sufferings of the cross that we are given to endure with His strength for our eternal benefit. We share in the sufferings of the whole Church because we are already united as the Body of Christ.

19. The Book of Lamentations was written in response to the destruction of Jerusalem, and specifically the temple. God allowed this terrible tragedy to happen, and Jeremiah does not step around that clear fact. God does not "willingly afflict or grieve" us; He would much rather shower us with His steadfast love that never ceases. Yet He allows us to suffer not as punishment for our sins but with the ultimate purpose that we would turn to Him and forsake our sins, trusting not in our stubborn love of evil but in His mercies that are new every morning.

20. Jesus quotes Isaiah 61 near the beginning of His ministry, as He preaches in the synagogue in Nazareth (Luke 4:16–21). He did not equivocate about this prophecy when He said, "Today this Scripture has been fulfilled in your hearing." The signs of evil—the valley of sorrow—include the poor, the brokenhearted, captives, the blind, those in prison, those who mourn, those of faint spirit, ruined cities long neglected, shame, and dishonor. Jesus, in His coming, delivers us from all of these evils and more, giving us the good news and release from the captivity of evil.

Day 5

21. When he wrote Philippians, Paul was likely in prison and facing certain death. As with everything he teaches, the apostle keeps Christ at the center of everything, even when he considers the end of his life. Since faith in the life-giving Savior is given in full, death for the Christian is considered gain. Departing this life to be with Christ is a far better way than to stay and suffer, yet God Himself will determine when the time is for each believer to leave this world.

22. Being at home in the body is walking by sight; it's paying too much attention to transient things that are built by human hands and will only waste away. To be at home in the body is to be away from the Lord, so it is detrimental to our faith. At home with the Lord is the proper perspective. It is governed by faith rather than sight; it sees bodily afflictions as slight and momentary, but necessary to prepare us for the great and heavenly glory that awaits us. We groan in this earthly tent of the body, not because we think we have no hope, but rather because we have a full desire for the salvation that we have been promised.

Example prayer: O Lord, our God, You have promised us the Holy Spirit as a guarantee of the rescue that is waiting for us in heaven. Put far away from us any desire to be at home in the body, grant us the faith that does not rely on sight, and fulfill in us the godly desire to please You, through Jesus Christ, our Lord. Amen.

23. A race is an agonizing experience in the moment, but then it comes to the end. The one who endures reaches the finish line with great joy and accomplishment. Those surrounding us are the saints who have by grace already finished the race, so they encourage us who are still running. We follow Jesus because it is His race. He won it for us already, so His joy that was fulfilled at the cross is given to us. When Paul uses the race image in Galatians, he mentions those who want to cut in, like a cheating opponent, so that we stumble. He was running as an apostle, and he wanted the other preachers of the Word to double-check his message of the Gospel so that the whole Church would "run" together well.

24. Christ's deliverance from evil is resurrection for our body and eternal life for our soul. Martha knew the promise was true that her brother Lazarus would rise again, but Jesus wanted her to know for certain that He *is* the resurrection and life. That means He not only talks about rising from the dead as some spiritual fact, but He also does it when He speaks the Word. He not only fulfills your life, but He actually gives life to you as a gift. When we pray for this twofold rescue from death, we can confidently say with Martha, "Yes, Lord; I believe."

25. Answers will vary. Experiences may touch on the despair that may have troubled the soul before the Lord's time of deliverance, the test of faith that could have helped rearrange some priorities that needed it, or how miraculous the rescue was that took place. Even though the urge during such events might be to "bargain" with God, such as promising to do something for Him if He'll get you out of this jam, this is not always a beneficial thing. Students may recall the crisis that drove Martin Luther from studying law to entering the monastery. That must have taught the reformer for the rest of his life to trust in the Lord for salvation rather than in man.

Amen: The Last Word?

Selected Passages

Preparing for the Session

Central Focus

Every "amen" accentuates the confidence and divine gift that prayer is. To conclude our study, this lesson traces the use of the word in the Bible, including when Jesus says, "Amen, amen" (ESV: "Truly, truly"). Students will be encouraged to extend prayer into a pattern of a uniquely Christian life lived in true and confident faith.

Objectives

That participants, led by the Holy Spirit working through God's Word, will

1. find out how the word *amen* is used in the Bible;
2. learn how both requests and thanksgivings work together in prayer; and
3. build a life of prayer that goes above and beyond mere words.

For the Small-Group Leader

Small-Group Discussion Helps

Day 1

1. With the exception of one instance (Psalm 106), each of these psalms end with a double Amen: "Amen and Amen." Perhaps this indicated an antiphonal chanting of this important word, that is to say, it could be that the leader of worship would say "Amen," and the people would respond the same. Also, these psalms are each the last ones in their "books," so the singing of "Amen" came as part of a doxology to close out each division in the Psalter. What is curiously missing is the Amen that we would have expected at the end of Psalm 150.

2. The covenant that the Lord made with Israel included a list of blessings for obedience as well as curses for specific sins against the covenant. This section in Deuteronomy specifies certain sins that violate God's covenant and deserve a curse if the people engage in these sins. The "Amen" that the people say to each curse not only shows their agreement but also calls down that very curse on the heads of transgressors. We could equate this with the practice of placing one's left hand on the Bible while raising the right hand in swearing an oath.

3. "The righteous shall live by his faith" is an Old Testament verse that is repeated more than once in the New Testament. Both what declares us just in God's sight and that which gives us life are brought about by God's faithfulness to us. By His grace, we believe His firm truth, and a way to express that rock-solid belief that no one can take away from us is to say, "Amen"—yes, it shall be so.

4. When the people say "Amen" at the end of this song of thanksgiving, they are voicing their praise to the Lord for all of the preceding mighty works: making known His name, bringing rejoicing to the faithful heart, rendering His judgments, remembering His covenant, defending them from enemies, spreading His Word to all nations, causing the heavens and earth to rejoice, and causing His steadfast love to endure forever. The occasion was the return of the ark of the covenant to the tent for which David was responsible, reclaiming the public place set aside as holy to the Lord and available to all God's people to seek the Lord's forgiving presence. A similar event today would be the dedication, re-dedication, or anniversary of a church building or congregation's founding.

5. The Lord neither contradicts His own identity nor goes back on what He says to us that He will do. His covenants are rich in one-way promises that we gratefully receive from His generous hand. Our heavenly Father freely binds Himself to do for us exactly as He promised, and He is delighted when in confident prayer we "pin Him down" to the very pledges that He gave to His people. In this way, "to a thousand generations," that is, for a time beyond our brief human reckoning, He will be pleased to ensure to us that He is ever-faithful, firm, and true to His covenant. Our "Amen" reveals to

Him and to one another the faith that He has given us to believe this.

Day 2

6. The Amen statements of Jesus (ESV: "Truly, I say to you") in these verses cover everything He came to do for our salvation, from the perfect fulfillment of the Law of Moses to the guarantee of paradise to the repentant thief on the cross. Along the way, He also uses the phrase to highlight the importance of a faith that is childlike, that firmly believes the powerful things that God is able to do, and that is willing to receive the Christ who comes to us as a servant.

7. Our Lord is especially adamant about faith, and so He warns about things that will harm that faith. The references from John 3 and 6 are not to be taken to mean that Baptism and feeding on Christ's flesh and blood are absolutely necessary as meritorious works to the exclusion of God's Word. Rather, they warn us that if we despise such precious gifts that are offered us by our Lord in the Word and Sacraments, then our faith and our hope in eternal life will suffer. Likewise, it is true with one who knowingly commits sin in a hardened, wickedly intentional way. Positively, to keep Jesus' Word is to be inoculated against eternal death. True faith enters heaven through Christ, the door for the sheep.

8. Jesus is the Word of God made flesh, as John teaches us in the first chapter of his Gospel. All other created things pass away, but Christ is the Word who abides forever. He went forth from the Father to accomplish His will for our salvation and ascended in a glorious return to heaven with a Holy Church that had been successfully purchased with His blood that was shed on the cross. When Jesus speaks, that is the living and active Word of God planting and watering our faith, piercing and yet also healing us by the work of the Holy Spirit.

9. When Christ finds a confident, unrelenting faith in the Canaanite woman, He is surprised not only that she would compare herself to a dog, but also that she believed the promise of Jesus even when Jesus Himself seemed to have been casting her away. She couldn't have mustered this faith on her own. God's Word was solely responsible for the magnificent trust that she had in Jesus' ability to heal. When we pray, we can be encouraged by this Gospel that, although we will face times when we feel convinced that our prayers are going unanswered, nevertheless our Savior loves us and has promised that our prayer is answered already.

10. The express purpose of this parable is for Jesus' disciples to pray continually and not lose heart, that is, not to quit praying because of despair over an apparent lack of the answer they want. Jesus asks the question about when He returns, "Will He find faith on earth?" and the answer is found in the fruits of that faith; among these would be faithful prayer that entrusts everything to God. We demonstrate that we believe the Lord's promise with full assurance when we say "Amen" to God's Word of truth. This is not by our own reason or strength at any time, but rather on account of the Lord's work that is done in our life of sanctification.

Day 3

11. Jesus had just cursed the fig tree to inspire faith in His disciples. He then granted it directly by telling them, "Have faith in God." The kind of faith that our Lord bestows on us is the faith that prays and believes so confidently that we have already received it. Hand in hand with praying and believing is the ability to forgive, and Jesus advises that, even as we pray, we would do well to grant that forgiveness to others without delay. All of this is not a demand on us, but rather informs us what He has already given.

12. God's promises to us find their Yes; that is, they become perfectly fulfilled in the perfect life, death, and resurrection of Jesus. He does not vacillate back and forth in accomplishing His will among us. That may be sometimes what our experiences make it look like, but Christ and what He has done make all promises happen for us. Just as God's gifts and blessings come to us through Christ, so it is also through Him working in us that we utter our response of faith that this blessing is indeed ours: Amen!

13. Revelation 5 includes "Amen!" as a word of liturgical worship, just like what we studied in the Old Testament. It is a final affirmation and answer to all the previous statements of worship that had been offered to the Lamb, Jesus Christ. The heavenly scene of chapters 4 and 5 have several elements of our Divine Service in them, and it gives us a sense that we are not alone as we gather on Sunday morning, but that we are joining "with angels and archangels and with all the company of heaven." The four living creatures, which traditionally have been assigned as symbols for each of the four Gospels, are the ones who say "Amen!" which could then affirm for us how Scripture inspires us to believe in and praise the Lord.

14. The apostle John says repeatedly that what he is inspired by the Holy Spirit to write is given specifically to generate and sustain faith in the promise of eternal life in Christ, the Son of God. To "know" means more than having the facts down; if that were all it was, then John should have written more signs and sayings of Jesus than he did. But knowing in spiritual matters means more: it means for you as a Christian to become inwardly convinced by the power of the Lord that eternal life is your possession. You demonstrate this confident faith by praying, that is, by calling on the name in which you have your life both now and forever.

15. As Revelation (and the whole Bible) draws to a close, Jesus leaves a parting promise of His second and final coming. Some comforting truths about this certainty include vindication over our spiritual enemies; Jesus as beginning and end, Alpha and Omega; the right to the tree of life restored (a return to an even better Eden); the Christian's enjoyment of Jesus' return as a bride rejoices to see her bridegroom; admission into the New Jerusalem; and drinking freely from the water of life. *Example prayer:* O Lord Jesus, You promise to come again soon. Grant that I may not grow weary in waiting for Your salvation, but that I would pray with confidence, speak to others with boldness, and control my sinful nature's urges with diligence. Amen.

Day 4

16. When we are convinced that the Lord is right there among us, then by faith we can truly rejoice in His presence. It's not that we have a disciplinarian staring over our shoulders, forcing us to do what He wants. Rather, it is our wonderful Savior who is there, guiding us all the way. "The Lord is at hand" also refers to His coming in glory, to which the Christian looks forward in expectation, praying and living as though He were to come down out of heaven the very next minute. Paul emphasizes it because we, too, are often borne down with the things that discourage us. It is not our power, but the Holy Spirit's, that gives us the ability to rejoice.

17. Jesus says He will be with us always. He is true God and true man, and He ever will remain so, even in heavenly glory. Being a man was never of itself a sign of humiliation for Him—it was God's plan from the beginning. Christ accomplishes His promise through what He commands here and elsewhere: Baptism and teaching the Word, not to forget also the body and blood of the Lord's Supper. At the end of the age, there will be no more need for His promise to be with us in our struggles on earth, because at that time we will be with Him in heaven!

18. The Song of Moses is the immediate response to the Israelites' miraculous rescue from Pharaoh in the Red Sea. They can see the dead bodies for themselves, and they know that God alone had a hand in delivering them. Not only the Egyptians but also all the enemies of God's people will tremble at the news of His mighty power. Moses and those who sing with him now call upon the Lord and His holy majesty to bring them through to their own land, to fulfill the promise that He has already made to their ancestors. The point of dwelling in the land is above all to make it a sanctuary of worship to the Lord and to establish His eternal reign, something that was fully accomplished at the cross and empty tomb.

19. While discussing the harmful effects of those who make arbitrary rules forbidding this and that, Paul tells Timothy that everything God created is good, and if it is received with thanksgiving, then it is consecrated (set aside as holy) by the Word of God and prayer. This does not constitute a method designed in any way to improve the object or person blessed, as if it were not good before. Instead, the good created things of God are—through our thankful prayer, grounded in Scripture—made holy for us also (to borrow a phrase from the Small Catechism).

20. Paul calls for watchfulness in prayer, because as we found, we need to be ever on guard against spiritual attack. We also are called upon to pray as the Word of God goes forth throughout the world and around the block. Mission is an essential activity both of the apostles and of the Church today. Prayer is vital to the success of mission work, as long as that success is measured in the perspective of God and His Word, rather than our worldly standards. Paul and his associates were mighty servants of God, yet they knew their strength came not from within themselves, but from above, so they constantly beseeched prayers, even from the most novice of Christians.

Day 5

21. Joshua was commanded, and by God's grace also enabled, to be strong and courageous, as he took over the leadership of Israel from Moses to guide them into the Promised Land. Prayer would be an integral part of his life and vocation, because the Book of the Law, that is, the Lord's perfect instruction for His people, would not

depart from Joshua's lips. He would read it, meditate on it (say it repeatedly to himself), and call upon the promises that God swore to their fathers.

22. Paul had said, "The life I now live in the flesh I live by faith in the Son of God" (Galatians 2:20). In this way of looking at it, our life under grace, washed through Baptism in the forgiveness of sins paid for by the blood of Christ, is offered to God as a prayer that is pleasing to Him. The Christian's daily work in his several God-given vocations can be thought of as an act of prayer and worship. Combined with the actual prayers, and partaking of gifts in the Divine Service, a believer's life most certainly is a faithful prayer too. Where this statement can get misunderstood is if it were to provide some excuse not to pray, that some "requirement" to pray is fulfilled just by living as a nominal Christian. In that case, faith would be stifled because the Law is crowding out the Gospel.

23. The natives of Malta were evidently very familiar with the might of the sea, and they attributed concepts such as justice to beings much higher than they. Their devotion to their various gods was so strong that they interpreted all their experiences in light of what they worshiped. At first, Paul was among those rescued from the sea, yet because he was bitten by a viper, it seemed to make sense to his island hosts that he was a murderer. But when, by the power of God, the snake's venom had no effect on Paul, the Maltese readily changed their mind to the opposite: he must have been a god. Would that our faith—the true faith at that—might influence our way of looking at our world around us a little more!

24. Jude wrote most of his short epistle to warn his fellow Christians about how difficult the task would be "to contend for the faith" (v. 3). Now, in the closing verses, he commends them to the almighty power of the Lord. He is able to keep us from stumbling, for stumble we will, also in our privilege of prayer. We are confident to approach His throne of grace in prayer because God Himself will present us blameless before His throne of glory. The One who offers this to us is the God who came into our human flesh and who now in that glorified flesh possesses all majesty, power, and dominion, now and forever. We pray because we know the guy who's in charge!

25. Encourage students to share answers and discuss prayer's role in their Christian life. Take note of improvements and needs for encouragement, and include them in your personal thanksgivings and petitions. Stress with students how important it is to consider prayer not as a duty but a privilege, not as a way to get things out of God, but an acknowledgement that we have everything in Christ already.